PROBATION CASEWORK

The Convergence of Theory with Practice

Joan Luxenburg

UNIVERSITY
PRESS OF
AMERICA

LANHAM • NEW YORK • LONDON

University Press of America,™ Inc.

4720 Boston Way
Lanham, MD 20706

3 Henrietta Street
London WC2E 8LU England

Library of Congress Cataloging in Publication Data

Luxenburg, Joan, 1948–
   Probation casework.

   Bibliography: p.
   1. Probation officers–United States–Case studies.
2. Professional socialization–United States–Case studies.
3. Probation–United States–Case studies. I. Title.
HV9278.L89   1983   364.6'3'0973   83–4845
ISBN 0–8191–3270–5
ISBN 0–8191–3271–3 (pbk.)

To Margaret, my first supervisor at the "Metropolitan
Area Department of Probation"

Acknowledgements

The author is appreciative to a committee of four who critiqued the study in its dissertation stage. Thanks to Geroge Z. F. Bereday, Joseph C. Grannis, Francis A. J. Ianni, and Rozanne Marel for their helpful comments. Also, thanks to anonymous reviewers (provided by University Press of America) for other helpful suggestions.

Appreciation is extended to my colleagues, Frank Cullen and Lloyd Klein, for their continuous encouragement and support given to me. I also wish to thank Alfred R. Lindesmith for sustaining in me a belief in the importance of qualitative analysis.

Special thanks are extended to my friend, Bob Smith, for proofreading the final manuscript.

CONTENTS

Preface

In this case study of a large urban area's probation department, the priority, method, and outcome of the probation-supervision process were examined and discussed in relation to six selected major theories of socialization (psychoanalytic, self-other, cognitive-developmental, classical conditioning, operant conditioning, and social learning).

The stated goals of the study were the following: (1) to intellectualize the role of a probation officer; (2) to show the probation-supervision process as an educative or reformative one, e.g., a system that resocializes lawbreakers; (3) to identify the dominant method of socialization relied upon by the probation-supervision process; (4) to formulate the probation-supervision model, accounting for its priorities, as well as for its limitations in outcome; (5) to provide illustrations (through case histories) of the application of the probation-supervision model; and (6) to perform the therapeutic contribution of "reflectation" upon the potential client (referred to in pseudonym as the "Metropolitan Area Department of Probation"). The sixth goal, that of "reflectation," is an exercise in reflection and interpretation for the purpose of potentially confronting the probation department with inconsistencies in its performance.

Ten case histories of adult criminal probationers were obtained through the use of a purposive sample. The writer had been employed as a Metropolitan Area probation officer during a six-year period from 1969 through 1975. Cases were selected from the writer's actual caseloads; however, names of persons and other identifying labels were changed in order to preserve the anonymity of the subjects. The exercise in combining the methodologies of participant observation and case history presentation is addressed in the study with reference to the issues which can complicate the interpretation and use of the data. The ten offender types chosen for illustrative purposes were the following: (1) sociopathic offender (rapist/larcenist), (2) robber, (3) assaultist repeater, (4) auto thief repeater, (5) white collar criminal (employee theft), (6) drug addict (heroin), (7) drug addict (methadone), (8) nonviolent sex offender, (9) statutory rapist, and (10) intoxicated driver repeater.

Through case history presentation, coupled with brief analyses of the cases, the description of the

xi

probation-supervision process was sustained as one that conforms to an interdependent network of priority, method, and outcome. The probation-supervision process has been described by the writer as a system which allocates greater priority to the probationer's demonstration of expected behavior than it allocates to the probationer's acquisition of the expected values underlying the behavior. Further, the probation-supervision process has been described as a system which relies heavily upon reinforcement as its method to induce obedience on the part of the probationer. The consequent outcome of the probation-supervision process has been described as a system which fosters opportunistic (or superficial) learning.

The study includes references to organizational constraints which were found by the writer within the Metropolitan Area Department of Probation. Excessive size of caseloads and limited opportunity for behavioral encounters between probation officers and their probationers are factors which have been discussed or alluded to by the writer as part of the reflectation goal of the study.

When properly viewed in a nonthreatening manner, the seemingly critical commentary on resocialization efforts is not put forth as an exposé on probation services. The study is intended as a reflection upon and an interpretation of the probation officer's role performance--an exercise in self-confrontation from which probation personnel can benefit.

As a text, the study can be a valuable aid to students of casework. The case analyses have been purposely kept brief, so as to offer the reader an opportunity to use his/her own skills in analyzing the cases. As illustrations, the cases can serve to stimulate classroom discussion on how to apply such casework techniques as: interviewing, data collection, making referrals, setting initial goals, contracting, evaluating goal attainment, terminating contact, etc.

Understandably, no two probation officers are likely to give a case the same exact treatment. However, their diversity of contacts is guided by principles of casework that reflect common understandings of professional responsibility. In adhering to the National Association of Social Worker's code of ethics, the practitioner may find contradictory expectations among one's obligation to self, client, colleagues,

employing agency, the profession, and society. These
contradictions are the challenges of casework; and
their successful resolutions are the rewards.

Chapter I

INTRODUCTION

The task which the writer has undertaken is to intellectualize the role of a probation officer. This analysis is seldom attempted, least of all by the probation officer involved first-hand in the field. The intention is to go beyond mere case analysis to evaluate probation supervision as a change agent. There is a need to view probation-supervision efforts as educative ones. There is a concern with the societal mechanisms that educate or socialize individuals into law-abiding behavior. Where obstacles block the goal of norm commitment, the writer presents an opportunity to view a societal microsystem which proposes to resocialize individuals who, by societal standards, have proved to be failures in adopting societal rules for behavior.

The discussion becomes more specific later, as to the actual social-psychological processes involved in the strategy of the probation officer as a potential agent of resocialization. However, for introductory purposes here, a condensed personal description of the probation officer's duties will be provided. Who become probation officers; what is their function; where do they perform; when do they become involved; why do they act; and, last but not least, how do they operate? These questions will be quickly answered here, but are elaborated upon throughout the work and do in fact constitute the entire effort of intellectualizing the role of a probation officer.

Who Become Probation Officers?

The writer served as a probation officer in a large city, which will be referred to as "Metropolitan Area." This pseudonym for the work location is being used to protect the privacy of the office in which the participant-observation data were gathered. The writer worked as a probation officer in Metropolitan Area during the period of October, 1969 to October, 1975. Qualifications for probation officers in Metropolitan Area are comparable to minimum job prerequisites for probation officers in large metropolitan areas throughout the United States. In smaller communities, qualifications become more lax, adjusted to the local talent pool. At the time of this writer's appointment, there were three ways in which to meet the hiring standards

1

of Metropolitan Area. A potential candidate for the job could be appointed by his/her ranked test score on a civil service exam after an interview, providing the candidate had passed his/her twenty-first birthday. His/her educational and vocational experience had to fall within one of the following three categories: (1) possession of a B.A. degree with a minimum of twenty-four credits in the behavioral sciences, plus two years of prior casework experience; or (2) in lieu of the two years of prior casework experience, possession of a relevant M.A. degree, e.g., in the behavioral sciences, education, or social work; or (3) in lieu of both the two years of prior casework experience and the possession of a relevant M.A. degree, two years of probation-officer traineeship (with the title of "probation-officer trainee"). The motivation of those who take the job is varied, but usually revolves around their prior studies in the behavioral sciences.

While a description of the social and character traits of the staff with whom this writer interacted is tempting to pursue here, the writer is in a difficult position to do so. There existed a variety of personality types among co-workers, ranging from the very dedicated to the indifferent. Undoubtedly, the individual personalities of probation personnel affect their job performance. However, in making observations of the probation-supervision process, attention has been directed to collecting data about the departmental procedures, not data on the sociological attributes of those persons carrying out the job performance. A sociogram of the office in which the writer worked would have been illustrative of both positive and negative aspects affecting the probation-supervision process.

What Is Their Function?

Probation officers are vested with several areas of responsibility. Usually a job assignment at any specific time confines the probation officer to one purpose. Either he/she investigates for the purpose of recommending court actions (dispositions or sentences) or he/she supervises individuals who have been discharged to him/her by the courts. Either he/she works with Family Services (e.g., juveniles) or he/she works with Adult Services. In Family Services, he/she can occupy the status of an intake officer, screening complaints to decide whether or not an actual petition should be drawn up. At times, all of the above serv-

2

ices can be performed by one probation officer, if he/she works in a multi-functional setting. This writer had the opportunity to work in such a setting, thereby being able to perform the following list of functions under one job assignment:
1. Criminal Court presentence investigations (including compiling social histories and making recommendations for sentencing);
2. Criminal Court supervision (counseling) of adults placed on probation;
3. Family Court enforcement of child suport and alimony orders (including settling disputes over visitation and assaultive behavior);
4. Family Court adoption investigations;
5. Family Court custody investigations;
6. Family Court Child Abuse and Child Neglect investigations;
7. Family Court supervision of Child Abuse and Child Neglect cases;
8. Family Court juvenile delinquency predispositional investigations (including seeking placement facilities for those in need);
9. Family Court supervision (counseling) of juvenile delinquency cases;
10. Family Court investigation of "Persons In Need of Supervision" cases (e.g., incorrigibility, truancy, etc., including seeking placement facilities for those in need);
11. Family Court supervision (counseling) of Persons In Need of Supervision cases.
The writer had a unique opportunity to have a multipurpose caseload involving all of the aforementioned functions in the course of a day's work. The discussion will focus on the one casework function that occupies the sole concern of this text--the supervision of adult criminal cases.

Upon becoming acquainted with the quantity of chores of the probation officer, the reader may have good cause to question the qualitative aspects of the probation officer's chores. The issue of qualitative casework will be addressed in Chapter III's discussion of organizational constraints.

Where Do They Perform?

In Metropolitan Area there was a probation branch-office attached to each Family Court, Criminal Court (misdemeanor cases), and Supreme Court (felony cases). In addition, there were two community-based,

3

multi-functional branches detached from the court setting. These were experimental and no longer exist. The one in which this writer was assigned remained in existence from June, 1969 to July, 1976. The work of the probation officer is done at his/her desk, in the courtroom, at home visits, at employment visits, and at visits to other agencies (e.g., schools, hospitals, drug programs, jail interview rooms, etc.). The nature of the particular case dictates where the probation officer makes his/her contacts. The case histories presented in Chapter IV will illustrate the varied settings in which the probation officer conducts his/her contacts.

When Do They Become Involved?

The supervision probation officer is assigned when the court imposes a disposition or a sentence of probation. The investigating probation officer is assigned after a finding of guilt (in adult cases) or after a "finding of fact" (in juvenile and other Family Court cases). Usually, if conditions permit, the investigating probation officer has approximately six weeks (longer in Supreme Court) to compile and verify the background information to present to the court. There are instances wherein the investigating probation officer may have one day in which to interview, verify what he/she can, and present a recommendation to the court. This writer has personally had to investigate and prepare a report to the court all in a period of one day.

Why Do They Act?

In the case of the investigating probation officer, he/she is seen by the court as a resource to gather information to help the court make a decision (a disposition or a sentence). It is not unusual to find two co-defendants (or two co-respondents in Family Court) each receive a separate type of sentence (or disposition). The rationale for the sentence or disposition depends upon the background (personal history, present functioning, attitude, etc.) of the individual, rather than the allegations that were sustained in the complaint or in the petition. Investigating probation officers, therefore, act to present information about the individual to the court with a recommendation for the specific type of treatment needed by the individual. The supervision probation officer acts to reintegrate the individual with the society from which the

4

individual has deviated. He/she acts in the hope that his/her intervention (diffused through appropriate agencies, if needed) will resocialize the individual. The premise is that incarceration is not necessary to accomplish the resocialization. Examples of this proposed intervention are provided later in the case histories contained in Chapter IV.

How Do They Operate?

The investigating probation officer consults official police records, court records, and the records of other appropriate agencies. He/she interviews the defendant (or respondent in Family Court) and members of the family. At one time, home visits and contacts with arresting officers and complainants were part of the Criminal Court investigation; but these have been eliminated due to the increasing volume of cases in Metropolitan Area. These practices are still conducted in Supreme Court and Family Court, especially the home visit. After compiling the facts and recommending a sentence in Criminal and Supreme Court cases, the work of the investigating probation officer is completed. In Family Court cases, often the process of searching for a placement facility for a youngster lingers on and, in the interim (which has been personally experienced by this writer to sometimes last as long as a period of a year and a half), the probation officer services the case almost as though it were under supervision.

With regard to the supervision probation officer, the question of how he/she operates is the crux of this study. How the probation-supervision process adheres to models of socialization and resocialization will constitute the framework of the study. In Chapter III the description of the probation-supervision model will have two points of primary concern to the reader. Firstly, the probation officer can rely only on changing overt behavior, since attitudes are internal states beyond his/her domain. Secondly, the relationship between the probation officer and the probationer is characterized primarily by authority and power on the probation officer's part and by a presumption of obedience on the part of the probationer. The latter signs an agreement before the court to abide by the orders and conditions of probation. He/she is aware that an infraction of the rules of probation can result in the probation officer's filing of a violation of probation. If there is a finding of guilt concerning

5

the violation of probation, the probationer is subject to resentencing at the recommendation of the probation officer. Thus, the probationer willingly consents at the time of his/her original sentencing to be subjected to the commands of his/her probation officer, so that the probationer can remain in the community, rather than enter confinement.

The aforementioned version of the probation officer's role has been presented to acquaint the reader with the probation officer as a component of the probation-supervision process. As the study proceeds, the image of the probation-supervision process becomes complete with detail and with the writer's interpretation of what has been observed of the process.

Purpose of The Study

The study was undertaken to examine the process of probation supervision of adult law-violators. The probation-supervision process will be viewed as a "resocializing" effort. The need to resocialize an adult implies that the socialization of this individual has failed in one or several areas. In a logical sequence, then, concern rests within three general topics:

A. Socialization;
B. Resocialization;
C. The Probation-Supervision Process.

Socialization

In Chapter II, the relevant sociological and psychological literature that defines the term "socialization" will be discussed. From this literature, the most relevant models of socialization will be presented. There will be no need to look for sharp contrasts separating the various models. As Pitrim Sorokin suggests, variations in definitions of the term "socialization" result from the idiosyncratic reasoning belonging to each theorist, rather than from actual differences existing in the meaning of the phenomenon.[1] Therefore, variations that are found in models of socialization are actually redundant in that they are not varying in their description of the phenomenon of socialization, but are placing emphasis on what each theorist finds to be of salience for his/her purposes. To illustrate the preceding statements, the models will be divided into two broad categories. These categories are actually polarities of a continuum, thus allowing for gradations between the categories and overlapping of the categories. One category emphasizes "internal mechanisms" of control in the acquisition of societal norms. The other category emphasizes "external mechanisms" in this acquisition. In other terms, one can refer to this continuum as a polarity between "individual" and "environment," the former being associated with internal mechanisms and the latter referring to external mechanisms. The reader will find that certain models speak of the etiology of faulty socialization as the product of the individual's failure, while other models will emphasize the environment's failure. Still a third and overlapping category speaks of a combination of individual and environmental failure. When an individual generates feelings of guilt within himself/herself having perceived that his/her conception of himself/herself differs from his/her conception of what society expects of him/her, he/she appears to be experiencing an internal mechanism of social control. He/she has accepted the expectations of society as his/her own expectations of himself/herself. This internalization differs from a response pattern based on environmental consequences (external mechanisms of social control). Similarly, when an individual feels anxiety after having transgressed what he/she knows to be a societal dictate, he/she may be said to be experiencing an internal mechanism of social control, providing that the anxiety is caused by his/her perceived discomfort with himself/herself. By contrast, when an individual experiences anxiety stemming from anticipated outside consequences (e.g., reprisals from others in the environment) for his/her transgressions of societal dictates, he/she may be said to be responding to an external mechanism of social control.

In Chapter II, the writer discusses and diagrams the individual/environment continuum, placing major theories of learning appropriately closer to the internal or external points of the continuum. The major theorists to be discussed in Chapter III are the following:
1. Sigmund Freud and Erik Erikson (psychoanalytic theory);[2]
2. Charles Horton Cooley and George Herbert Mead (self-other theory);[3]
3. Jean Piaget and Lawrence Kohlberg (cognitive-developmental theory);[4]
4. Ivan Pavlov (classical conditioning theory);[5]
5. B. F. Skinner (operant conditioning theory);[6]
6. Albert Bandura (social learning theory).[7]

7

Resocialization

The term "resocialization" is not to be thought of as a "separate" undertaking occurring after socialization has failed. All theoretical notions of socialization are in agreement that socialization is an on-going learning process that continues throughout one's lifetime. Therefore, resocialization takes place within the continued process of socialization.

Most of the researchers who turn their attention to the resocialization process are in what are referred to as "corrective" fields. The criminal corrections field, of course, is one very important of these, and receives the sole attention of the study. Other "corrective" fields include mental hygiene (e.g., therapeutic psychology, psychiatry, etc.) and medical rehabilitation through the use of drugs (e.g., to correct chemical and chromosomal imbalances, etc.).

In their book, Resocialization: An American Experiment, the authors, Daniel B. Kennedy and August Kerber, divide their concern into three "corrective" areas: (1) education (resocializing efforts directed toward human failures within the educational system, e.g., the underachiever); (2) industry (resocializing efforts directed toward human failures in the employment system, e.g., the hard-core unemployable); and (3) the criminolegal system (resocializing efforts directed toward human failures in the legal system, e.g., the criminal). The study will draw heavily upon the above authors' views on resocialization within the criminolegal setting.[8]

Kennedy and Kerber agree that resocialization is a phase of socialization; however, they present a model of the differences between the two phases. Their model,[9] shown in Table 1, will be elaborated upon in Chapter III in terms of relating the probation-supervision process to the right-hand side of the dichotomies with reference to both the "self" and the "agent."

8

TABLE 1

SOCIALIZATION VERSUS RESOCIALIZATION

	Self Socialization/ Resocialization	Agent Socialization/ Resocialization
Who	Tabula Rasa/ Accumulated Experiences	Primary Group/Secondary Group
What	Develop/Alter	Guide/Redirect
How	Dependent/Independent	Affective/Disaffective
Why	Natural Process/ Comply	Natural Process/Restore Equilibrium
When	Continuous/Sporadic	Continuous/Sporadic
Where	Natural Setting/ Artificial Setting	Natural Setting/ Artificial Setting

The Probation-Supervision Process

"Probation supervision" may be defined as a process whereby an individual who has been convicted of a crime is sentenced to a period of community surveillance and guidance (under the aegis of a court-appointed probation officer) in lieu of incarceration. Frances T. Cullen and Karen E. Gilbert, in their text, Reaffirming Rehabilitation, discuss the historical development and rationale for probation.[10] These authors explain that during the Progressive era (the first two decades of the 1900's), reformers emphasized individualized and community treatment approaches to corrections. Progressives urged the expansion of probation on two grounds--one which justified the supervision function, and the other, the investigative function. Firstly, probation supervision was expected to provide counseling by probation officers who would be sensitive, yet stern. Secondly, probation officers were needed to research a convicted defendant's background to provide recommendations to the court (presen-

9

tence reports) for a sound and appropriate treatment plan. These two separate functions remain in operation today and have not actually strayed from the good intentions of their early proponents. While the supervision function is the sole concern of this text, the reader will note that in the case histories (to be presented) the supervision plan is very dependent upon the preliminary investigative work conducted during the presentence report.

Martin Haskell and Lewis Yablonsky in their book, Criminology: Crime and Criminality, separate the four primary functions of the correctional system (and this system includes probation supervision).[11] These functions are: "protective" (the offender's behavior should be more or less closely supervised for a period of time); "punitive" (the offender should be deprived of some or all of his/her liberty for a period of time); "reformative" (the offender should experience some change in his/her values, attitudes, and behavior); and "rehabilitative" (the experience with the correctional system will result in less likelihood of the offender's violating laws). Because of Haskell and Yablonsky's distinction between the reformative and rehabilitative functions, the writer has chosen to work with the concept of the reformative function as equivalent to resocialization. The term "reformative" refers to modifying deviant behavior (and attitudes and values) toward acceptable societal standards. The phrase "rehabilitative function" connotes improving formal educational and vocational skills. This task has some relevance to socialization and resocialization, but is not sufficient by itself to constitute these processes.

In addition to the reformative aspect associated with resocialization, the writer is concerned with our society's arrangement of priorities in its initial and ongoing attempts to socialize individuals. A model of childhood and adult socialization which will be referred to in the study is presented by Orville G. Brim in his essay "Socialization Through the Life Cycle."[12] Table 2 is used by Brim[13] and will be used in Chapter III to formulate the model of the probation-supervision process.

Providing the individual with "ability" to be able to carry out expected behavior and uphold expected values (cells C and D) would be the equivalent concept of what the writer (and Haskell and Yablonsky) refers

10

to as "rehabilitation," while instilling "knowledge" of expected behavior and values (cells A and B), and more importantly--"motivation" or the desire to conform to expected behavior and the desire to pursue the expected values (cells E and F) would be the equivalent of what the writer (and Haskell and Yablonsky) refers to as "reformative."

TABLE 2

SOCIALIZATION THROUGH CHILDHOOD AND ADULTHOOD

	Behavior	Values
Knowledge	A	B
Ability	C	D
Motivation	E	F

Interestingly enough, Brim proposes that when we are considering childhood socialization, society places its highest priority in cell F, caring most that the child be motivated to hold acceptable values.[14] And when we are considering adulthood socialization, according to Brim, society places its highest priority in cell A, caring most that the adult "knows" (and therefore carries out) the expected overt behavior.[15] The question which inevitably will have to be dealt with in the assessment of the probation-supervision process is one which asks where the probation system places its priorities. For instance, where the probation-supervision process confirms Brim's thesis, the study's empirical question will deal with whether or not we are expecting individuals to conform to societal norms merely with the possession of the knowledge of and the motivation for expected behavior and values, when these individuals may not have the skills (ability) necessary to carry out the appropriate behavior and pursue the appropriate values. If the answer to this question is yes, then one might suggest that the probation system re-arrange its priorities.

In Chapter III, one finds the probation system's priorities, as well as its limitations. The latter

11

seem to dictate to the probation system what its priorities must be. A model is developed of the probation-supervision process as one that can operate with only observable behavior, is characterized by an obedience form of social influence, and has organizational inconsistencies that impede its goals. With these constraints placed upon the probation-supervision process, the outcome may be predicted to be superficial learning.

Procedure and Methodology

This study is a descriptive analysis of the probation-supervision process. Since the writer is relating the probation-supervision process to models of socialization that appear in the literature, Chapter II will present "library work" in the fields of sociology and psychology to cite the models of socialization that are being compared to the probation-supervision process. Two of these models have been explicitly referred to in the preceding section of this chapter. These were proposed by Brim and by Kennedy with Kerber. Other literature has been suggested also in the preceding section when the reference was made to perspectives of socialization that lie along the continuum of internal to external mechanisms of social control.

The primary methodology is that of participant observation. The object of study is the Metropolitan Area Department of Probation where this writer spent a six-year period (October, 1969 to October, 1975) employed as a probation officer, performing varied functions, one of which was the supervision of adults placed on probation. During this same six-year period, the writer's concomitant engagement in graduate study provided the presupposition that the probation experience was going to be documented for study. The specific formulation of the study was made during the writer's last two years with the probation department.

Because data come exclusively from the above experience, one must note the delimitations of the study by referring to it as a case study of the Metropolitan Area Department of Probation. Undoubtedly, variations of the probation-supervision process exist in other probation departments across the country. However, the comparative aspect of how probation departments function elsewhere is not within the scope of this study. The writer will refrain from any comments as to the typicality of the Metropolitan Area Department of

12

Probation. However, Metropolitan Area is one of the country's most heavily populated large urban centers. As such, its probation department can adequately represent what is referred to as the probation-supervision process. This statement is not to be construed as a statement that the department is representing probation departments elsewhere. It is representing what has been defined as probation supervision.

To structure the participant-observation method for presentation to the reader, case histories of offenders (with whom the writer has been involved) will be used. There is the inevitable factor of the writer's selectivity in choosing which of several case histories might best illustrate a certain type of offender. Because this text cannot include all of the cases with which the writer has worked over the six-year period, it is necessary to select. The most practical criterion for this selection is to choose those cases which contain the most data and which best illustrate the writer's perception of the probation-supervision model. It is worthy of notation here that the writer had kept her own hand-written copies of all case histories with which she had worked. These had been handed back to the writer by typists after each case had been typed. Therefore, the writer is not going to proceed by the use of selective memory; but will use selective relevance. In Chapter IV, before presenting the case histories, the rationale for selecting ten case histories will be discussed in detail. It will become clear that a purposive sample has been used. The question of whether the writer's first-hand contact with the case histories distorts the purpose for which they are being used within this study will also be addressed.

A classification of offender types is necessary to match case histories accordingly. Don C. Gibbons, a criminologist, presents a good typology for this purpose.[16] The writer will be referring to Gibbons' schema of fifteen categories of offenders, which Gibbons identifies through consideration of motives, personality, and behavior patterns peculiar to each type. The final categories will vary slightly from Gibbons' schema. One practical reason for this is that some of Gibbons' categories refer to felons, while the writer has worked only with misdemeanants. In addition, Haskell and Yablonsky and Marshall Clinard with Richard Quinney present categories of offender types, used by this writer to extend Gibbons' typology somewhat.[17]

Reliance is placed heavily upon Haskell and Yablonsky's schema, since it helps to justify society's concern for how treatment is to take place.

The Significance of and Justification for the Study: Its Contributions

There will be both theoretical and empirical benefits resulting from the study. Of primary significance is the exercise presented in participant-observation research of an institution of resocialization. While others have evaluated and drawn conclusions about the probation-supervision system, few have viewed it from the perspective of a practitioner (e.g., a probation officer, involved first-hand with the process).[18] The writer looks at the probation system from this perspective; and therefore adds to the literature provided by participant observers of case studies in the corrections field.

Previous studies that attempt to quantify the effects of probation-supervision as a resocializer present contradictory empirical data, probably due to their method of inquiry.[19] The following examples illustrate the point:

1. The Saginaw Probation Demonstration Project:[20] This study, conducted in 1963 in Michigan, worked with the well-agreed upon assumption that close, personal contact between probation officers and clients is related to a low rate of recidivism. Therefore, the experimental condition provided for small caseloads so as to allow probation officers to spend extensive time with clients. The results of the three-year study indicated that increased supervision resulted in a greater degree of resocialization.[21]

2. The San Francisco Project: A Study of Federal Probation and Parole:[22] This two-year study reported in 1969 no significant difference between rates of recidivism when the degree of personalized supervision of probationers was varied.[23]

3. The California Community Treatment Project:[24] This program which began in 1961 and has been periodically assessed over the years provides close supervision, small caseloads, and individualized treatment tailored to the needs of clients. Yet, the results are not conclusive as to whether progress is being made in this program more than progress would be made in an institutional setting.[25]

4. The California Probation Subsidy Program:[26] This study reported on by the Chamber of Commerce of

the United States announces success. The concept of subsidy provides counties with a grant of $4,000 for each of ten offenders not sent to a state institution. The resulting $40,000 (for each of ten offenders per 100,000 citizens in a county's population) is used by the local probation department to improve services at all levels. The reduced workload has shown a success such that evaluation "during the first two years of this program demonstrated that improved probation services can be given to five or six persons at the local level for each individual grant."[27] It should be noted that this particular report on the above program emphasizes a costs-benefits analysis of the community-based treatment argument. However, the emphasis on cost-analysis precluded any details on the follow-up behavior of probationers involved in the improved services brought about by the subsidy.

5. The Georgia Experiment:[28] Excerpts of this evaluation are presented in a September, 1977 issue of the <u>Law Enforcement Assistance Administration Newsletter</u>. The article, entitled "Caseload Has Little Impact on Recidivism," reports on the findings of Professor Jerry Banks of the Georgia Tech School of Industrial and Systems Engineering. According to Banks, probation officers do not necessarily do a better job when they are given fewer offenders to supervise. Surprisingly, the report suggests that sometimes there is evidence of increased recidivism when the workload is reduced.[29] "The report points out the nearly impossible task of ever really giving probationers intensive supervision and the futility of trying to relate caseload to chances for rehabilitation."[30] This study was conducted through a $93,530 grant from LEAA's National Institute of Law Enforcement and Criminal Justice. The data were gathered from forty-six state, county, and city probation offices in Georgia offering special, intensive probation projects.

The reader may wonder how reduced caseload fares when used by parole agencies, rather than probation agencies. Though the present study is not dealing with parole supervision, it is recognized that parole's community-based supervision function is in many respects analogous to the function of probation supervision. Parole supervision is afforded to offenders who have earned the privilege of early, conditional release from incarceration. Of interest is a series of studies evaluating the California Special Intensive Parole Unit (or SIPU).[31] Mark J. Lerner has made a summary state-

15

ment with regard to the SIPU studies. According to Lerner, SIPU "found that decreased caseloads do not decrease recidivism."[32] Lerner refers to the one exception found in the SIPU III study which:

> found that the reduced caseloads worked better in the northern than in the southern region of California. Administratively, the two regions were distinct, with a more "law enforcement oriented" parole staff in the north, hence a policy of high return to prison.[33]

Recognizing the fact that the present study is not judging the resocializing effort of the probation-supervision process by measures of recidivism, the study is not pursuing answers that the aforementioned studies were seeking. The study is implicitly judging the probation-supervision process, but by a different criterion. The test for inferred success rests on the degree of conformity of the probation-supervision process to already widely accepted models of socialization. Within this context, the study first contributes to the theoretical base of socialization literature when, in Chapter II, models are categorized along the continuum of internal versus external mechanisms of social control. What is performed by such categorization is a tightening or pulling together of the available literature to construct tools for later comparison and analysis. The models of socialization are categorized in order to compare these to the probation system for analysis of that system in Chapter III.

Secondly, a new model of socialization will be contributed, drawn from a combination of variations that the probation system takes from already existing models. There will be areas in which one cannot find conformity when comparing the probation-supervision process to models of socialization. To reconcile the lack of conformity, the study must blend the conforming aspects with the nonconforming ones to construct a new model of socialization ("after the fact")--the one to which the probation system has been adhering unbeknownst to the practitioners. The empirical contribution in Chapters III and IV, therefore, is to make it known to those in the field exactly which model they are using. With an awareness of the model that the probation system is working with, it follows that probation officers can put their efforts in congruence with the model.

The latter contribution, referred to above, is roughly analogous to the one made by counselors and psychotherapists when they apply the technique known as "reflectation."[34]   First, the therapist "reflects" upon what the client has said, e.g., restating the client's exact thoughts, by paraphrasing without changing or adding to the original meaning. Then, the therapist uses "interpretation," by hypothesizing relationships about that which the client has spoken and about how the client has behaved. At this point, the therapist subjects the above to the client for the client's own consideration. In the analogy, the writer is first restating the literature on socialization ("reflecting" upon it). Then the writer is "interpreting" relationships between (a) what this literature suggests along with what the theory of probation-supervision suggests and (b) how the probation system actually operates. In Chapter V, the end result of this form of "reflectation" is to confront the probation system (the potential "client") with discrepancies and ways of reconciling these in order to identify a system's clouded reality. The system, very much like the therapist's client, should afterwards be prepared to cope with its newly acquired self-image.

Notes

[1]Pitrim Sorokin, Fads and Foibles in Modern Sociology (Chicago: Henry Regnery Co., 1956), pp. 3-20.

[2]Sigmund Freud's division of the superego into the "ego ideal" (which offers a standard of excellence) and the "conscience" (which generates feelings of guilt to inhibit the impulsive id) is often neglected. However, this division is acknowledged in Arlyne Lazerson, ed., Psychology Today: An Introduction (New York: Random House, 1975), pp. 217, 409, 423; Erik H. Erikson, Childhood and Society, 2nd ed. (New York: W. W. Norton & Co., 1963), pp. 247-74.

[3]Charles Horton Cooley, Human Nature and the Social Order (New York: Scribner's, 1902); George Herbert Mead, Mind, Self, and Society (Chicago: University of Chicago Press, 1934).

[4]Jean Piaget, The Moral Judgment of the Child, trans. M. Gabain (New York: Harcourt Brace Jovanovich, 1932); Lawrence Kohlberg, "Moral Stages and Moralization: The Cognitive-Development Approach," in Moral Development and Behavior: Theory, Research, and Social Issues, ed. Thomas Lickona (New York: Holt, Rinehart & Winston, 1976), pp. 31-55.

[5]Ivan Pavlov's classical conditioning sequence can be applied to the learning of morality through the process of "vicarious classical conditioning," pairing a previously neutral stimulus with a stimulus that evokes anxiety.

[6]B. F. Skinner's operant conditioning applied to moral development relies on rewards and punishments contingent upon and following the presented behavior, serving to increase desirable behavior and to decrease undesirable behavior.

[7]Albert Bandura (and other social learning theorists) discuss the role of imitation through mere observation of models or through observing the behavior and consequences of the model, as well as through receiving direct rewards and punishments. See Albert Bandura, Principles of Behavior Modification (New York: Holt, Rinehart & Winston, 1969).

[8]Daniel B. Kennedy and August Kerber, Resocialization: An American Experiment (New York: Behavioral Publications, 1973).

[9]Ibid, p. 44.

[10]Francis T. Cullen and Karen E. Gilbert, Reaffirming Rehabilitation (Cincinnati: Anderson Publishing Co., 1982), pp. 77-78.

[11]Martin R. Haskell and Lewis Yablonsky, Criminology: Crime and Criminality 2nd ed., (Chicago: Rand McNally, 1978), pp. 507-516.

[12]Orville G. Brim, Jr., "Socialization Through the Life Cycle," in Socialization After Childhood, ed. Orville G. Brim, Jr., and Stanton Wheeler (New York: John Wiley & Sons, 1966), pp. 3-49.

[13]Ibid., p. 25.

[14]Ibid., pp. 26-27.

[15]Ibid.

[16]Don C. Gibbons, Changing the Lawbreaker: The Treatment of Delinquents and Criminals (Englewood Cliffs, N.J.: Prentice-Hall, 1965), pp. 98-125.

[17]Haskell and Yablonsky (in their text previously cited) divide laws into five categories, leaving room to fit "criminal types" into the categories. Marshall B. Clinard and Richard Quinney, Criminal Behavior Systems: A Typology (New York: Holt, Rinehart & Winston, 1973), pp. 14-21.

[18]Kennedy (in Kennedy and Kerber) is viewing the probation-supervision method from his first-hand experience in the field.

[19]Ibid., p. 109.

[20]Michigan Council on Crime and Delinquency, The Saginaw Probation Demonstration Project (Lansing: Michigan Council on Crime and Delinquency, 1963).

[21]Ibid., pp. 32-34.

[22]University of California School of Criminology, The San Francisco Project: A Study of Federal Probation and Parole, Research Report no. 14 (Los Angeles: University of California Press, 1969).

[23]Ibid., pp. 6-9.

[24]U. S. Department of Health, Education, and Welfare, Children's Bureau, Children, "Alternatives to Institutionalization," by Marguerite Q. Grant and Martin Warren (Washington, D. C.: Government Printing Office, 1963). Information on the Community Treatment Project is included here although the C.T.P. is a part of the California Youth Authority, dealing with juvenile delinquents.

[25]Ibid.

[26]Chamber of Commerce of the United States of America, Marshaling Citizen Power to Modernize Corrections, reprinted by American Correctional Association (College Park, MD.: American Correctional Association, 1972), pp. 9-10.

[27]Ibid., p. 10.

[28]"Caseload Has Little Impact on Recidivism," Law Enforcement Assistance Administration Newsletter, 6 September 1977, p. 11.

[29]Ibid.

[30]Ibid.

[31]The California Adult Authority has published its self-reports in 1953, 1955, 1956, 1958, 1962, 1963, and 1965. The program's various phases were assessed by the State of California.

[32]Mark J. Lerner, "The Effectiveness of a Definite Sentence Parole Program," Criminology 15 (August, 1977): 213.

[33]Ibid.

[34]For more information on the term "reflectation" see Lawrence M. Brammer and Everett L. Shostrom, Therapeutic Psychology, 3rd ed. (Englewood Cliffs, N.J.: Prentice-Hall, 1977), pp. 254-271.

Chapter II

SOCIALIZATION THEORY

In this chapter a discussion of socialization literature is presented. The purpose is twofold. Firstly, there is a need to separate the previously mentioned categories of internal versus external mechanisms of social control. In accomplishing the categorization, the intent is not to polarize intrinsic motivation (to norm commitment) from its counterpart, extrinsic motivation. However, it is important to first show these extremes, and then recognize that, as processes, the two are not mutually exclusive. There is a third category mediating between the two, neither entirely intrinsic nor completely extrinsic. Additionally, throughout the categorization gradations are present. Therefore, there is actually a continuum wherein some theories of socialization approximate the intrinsic polarity (or rely solely on it), while other theories of socialization approximate the extrinsic polarity (or rely solely on it).

In becoming concerned with the above-mentioned continuum one can identify the theory of socialization which is closest to the theoretical base upon which the probation-supervision process relies. In Chapter III the probation-supervision process is formulated as a model. In doing so, one requires an element in the model that speaks distinctly of the method of social control relied upon by the process. In order to choose that element for inclusion in the model, it becomes practical to separate models of socialization according to the internal and external mechanisms that have already been defined in Chapter I. Secondly, the discussion of socialization literature presented here will serve as a backdrop for the forthcoming specific description of resocializing the offender. Before specifically interpreting the method of probation-supervision as a resocialization process, it is appropriate to define the terms socialization and resocialization. Having already acquainted the reader with the therapeutic contribution of "reflectation," the current chapter is presented as the "reflection" portion of the analysis--before the actual "interpretation," and before the actual blending of the two for "reflectation."

The actual reflectation will be completed in Chapter V. Reflecting is the subject of this chapter. Therefore, the relevant socialization literature will be repeated here. Redundancy in this form, as well as the reflecting performed in actual therapy, has a purpose in serving to clarify. The reflection is extended further into Chapter III where the client's expressed thoughts are repeated. The client is the Metropolitan Area Department of Probation, although social work practitioners would recognize the Metropolitan Area Department of Probation as a "potential client," since the agency did not request the therapeutic services.[1]

"Interpretation" (the second component of reflectation) is the process of suggesting existing relationships between such thoughts and actions as the client's actual behavior. When a "hypothesis" such as this is then used for the purpose of confronting the client with any discrepancies, the reflectation has been completed. The interpretation portion of the analysis will be presented in Chapters III and IV.

This present chapter has been identified as the one in which the reader can reflect upon the selected socialization literature. This is not a "review of the literature." One cannot cover here every theory in the literature; nor can one do each theory justice in the brief treatment of each.[2] The writer can, however, distinguish each major theory from the other, as well as show similarities where these exist. Those theories that have been selected appear to cover every broad approach to the concept of socialization. These approaches have already been cited in Chapter I as the psychoanalytic, the self-other, the cognitive-developmental, the classical conditioning, the operant conditioning, and the social learning. The writer will refer to the works of the leading exponents of each: Sigmund Freud and Erik Erikson for the psychoanalytic, Charles H. Cooley and George Herbert Mead for the self-other, Jean Piaget and Lawrence Kohlberg for the cognitive-developmental, Ivan Pavlov for the classical conditioning, B. F. Skinner for the operant conditioning, and Albert Bandura for the social learning.[3]

The Psychoanalytic Approach

Sigmund Freud's three components of personality are the id, ego, and superego.[4] The id represents an unconscious impulsive, uninhibited, egocentric, amoral, extremely hedonistic state of "pre-development." The id contains the sexual energies (libido) and the life and death wishes (eros and thanatos). It is governed by the "pleasure principle" and seeks immediate grati-

22

fication. The ego is governed by the "reality principle." It serves as a mediator between the id and the superego. It functions to postpone immediate gratification for long-range goals. The superego is composed of the "ego ideal" and the "conscience." The ego ideal represents societal standards for behavior (what we ought to do). We strive for perfection of these standards, if the ego ideal has developed. The conscience represents what we ought not to do. If the conscience is well-developed, guilt feelings emanate from that portion of the superego when we know that we have transgressed a societal dictate that we have come to internalize. An overdeveloped id and an underdeveloped conscience represent an unsocialized person or one who is not yet fully accepting of society's standards as his/her own.

Freud also contributed a scheme of stages of psychosexual development.[5] Erik Erikson, working in the tradition of psychoanalytic theory (emphasizing the unconscious), proposed a theory of eight stages of human development.[6] Progression through these stages is associated with adaptation to physiological changes being experienced and social responses being received. Each stage presents a crisis in need of resolution in the formation of identity. Erikson's eight stages appear below:

1. Trust versus Mistrust;
2. Autonomy versus Shame or Doubt;
3. Initiation versus Guilt;
4. Industry versus Inferiority;
5. Identity versus Role Confusion;
6. Intimacy versus Isolation;
7. Generativity versus Stagnation;
8. Integrity versus Despair.

Only the first four will be elaborated upon, as these are believed to be decisive in engendering feelings of competence in early years.[7] Competence becomes an important part of the definition of socialization to be presented after the discussion of the major theories.

Trust versus Mistrust

This stage is equivalent to Freud's psychosexual stage of oral development. The infant looks for nurturance and a warm responsiveness to its crying and to its need for oral gratification. If the caretaker (usually the mother) responds with food and cuddling quickly, warmly and consistently, a sense of trust toward the caretaker is likely to result. That feeling

23

of trust is likely to be generalized toward others in society at large. If the caretaker fails to respond quickly, warmly and consistently, the infant becomes distrusting of the caretaker and may generalize this attitude toward the rest of society.

Autonomy versus Shame or Doubt

This stage is equivalent to Freud's anal stage. Here the child is concerned with his/her own accomplishments, particularly those related to new motor skills. Self-control can be learned and demonstrated through bodily eliminations, e.g., retaining or eliminating bladder or bowel matter. Toilet training conducted in a nonthreatening atmosphere can help the child to gain confidence in his/her ability to control. If this ability to control is stifled by the caretaker, the child may develop a sense of shame about the act, and may in turn generalize this feeling to other situations. On the other hand, if the child is given carte blanche with regard to how much control he/she may exercise, he/she could become a discipline problem.

Initiative versus Guilt

In this stage the child begins to innovate, rather than merely imitate. Responses are coming from the caretaker and others, particularly peers during play. If peers (or the caretaker) show disapproving or indifferent reactions to the child's new mastery of the external, the child may hesitate to try new behavior. The child may punish himself/herself for what he/she perceives to be failure on his/her part. These feelings are the beginnings of guilt--recognizing self-initiated failure.

Industry versus Inferiority

In this stage the child begins to see the products of his/her labors at school and elsewhere. Mental and physical skill are being asked for in an impersonal setting. Failure is taken badly by the child. A fear of failure and its supposed consequences (the disdain of others) is felt. Avoidance of testing situations is a manifestation of feelings of inferiority.

The Self-Other Approach

Freud's contribution is the discussion of unconscious thought mechanisms. However, one cannot say that Freud's approach is divorced from a consideration of the self in relation to others. The ego ideal, as a construct, speaks of the societal standards. Here is the beginning of the taking into account the role of the organized "other" (society). Similarly, the interactions that Erikson speaks of are actually incidents of the "self" learning the perspective of the "other."

The theories which direct their attention to self-other systems are best expressed by Charles H. Cooley and George Herbert Mead.[8] Cooley contributed the concept of "the looking-glass self," arising from a social mirror-image. Specifically, Cooley refers to the development of one's self-image through feedback-- a reflected image that others have of the individual. According to Cooley, we see ourselves as we think others see us. This involves our perception of others, their evaluation of us, and our premium placed upon the opinion of others. Others appraise us. We appraise their appraisals of us. There is room for error on our part as well as on the part of others. There exist the possibilities that others are misperceiving us and we are misperceiving them. Nonetheless, we may choose to take into account their evaluation of us. This process is reflected self-appraisal.

George Herbert Mead presents an extensive view of self-other systems. Mead defines three major components necessary for socialization. These are: (a) the "mind," (b) the "self," and (c) the "society." The mind is a necessary prerequisite to learning. It is capable of problem-solving, abstractions, and other cognitions. The mind makes use of the significance of symbols, such that language may have a universal comprehension. Attitudes and other derivatives of thinking occur through inner conversation in the mind. The "self" can be viewed partially as an organization of attitudes. Through the self, the individual can be both the subject and the object--both the actor and the observer of his/her actions. The individual can take the role of the other (the outsider) in viewing his/her own actions. The self arises through play and game, which provide opportunities for role-taking. The self consists of the "I" and the "Me." The "I" component provides the individual's uniqueness. The "Me" represents the universal aspect of the self. "Society" is a community of selves. Since the self has a perspective of its own, society is an organized composite of the perspectives of its member selves. As a whole, this organization of different perspectives has a unity and can, therefore, represent socially accepted attitudes.

For Mead, "symbolic interactionism" accounts for the achievement of socialization. Interaction between the self and others is facilitated through the use of symbols which have universal significance (language). In addition to possessing language skills, one has to be equally capable of putting himself/herself in the perspective of the other (role-taking). Through play and game, the individual comes to participate in a variety of roles. An organized set of "others" is formed as a construct (the "generalized other") and is used as a gauge in assessing appropriate behavior. "Significant others" are those persons who are closest to us and who have some degree of control over incentives, rewards, etc. Significant others help to influence our responses in much the same way that Edwin Sutherland had described in the process of "differential association."[9] They serve as feedback to us. Our internalization of their standards represents social control.

The Cognitive-Developmental Approach

One can see that Mead recognized the importance of the mind and its problem-solving ability as a prerequisite to socialization. Jean Piaget focused upon the cognitive capacity of the individual to perform intelligently in a variety of social situations.[10] Piaget categorized stages of cognitive development that are invariant and associated with age. Piaget identified two major categories of intellectual development: (1) sensorimotor intelligence (infancy to 18 months), and (2) conceptual intelligence (beginning at approximately 18 months). The conceptual stage is further divided into three separate stages: (a) the preoperational (intuitive) stage (18 months to age 7), (b) the concrete-operational stage (age 7 to age 11), and the stage of formal operations (beginning at approximately age 12). The sensorimotor period is prior to the development of language and symbols. These capacities are acquired during the preoperational stage. The ability to assume the role of the other is usually accomplished through game and play that can take place in the concrete-operational stage. However, abstract thought is not characteristic of the understanding that the child expresses during the concrete-operational stage. It is during the stage of formal operations that the formation of general principles can appear.

Lawrence Kohlberg, in formulating a stage theory of morality, became concerned with Piaget's contribution. According to Kohlberg, "while logical development is a necessary condition for moral development, it is not sufficient."[11] By making this statement, Kohlberg recognized that the degree of moral reasoning is partially dependent upon the degree of logical reasoning which the individual is capable of. Kohlberg identified additional elements of morality that come about after logical reasoning. These three additional elements are social perception (or social perspective, or role-taking); moral judgment; and moral behavior.

Kohlberg formulated six sequential stages of moral judgment contained within three major levels.[12] These appear in the chart in Table 3.

TABLE 3

KOHLBERG'S STAGES OF MORAL DEVELOPMENT

Level	I	Preconventional
Stage 1		Heteronomous Morality
Stage 2		Individualism, Instrumental Purpose, and Exchange

Level	II	Conventional
Stage 3		Mutual Interpersonal Expectations, Relationships, and Interpersonal Conformity
Stage 4		Social System and Conscience

Level	III	Postconventional or Principled
Stage 5		Social Contract or Utility and Individual Rights
Stage 6		Universal Ethical Principles

With regard to who occupies which of the stages, Kohlberg has placed "most children under age 9, some adolescents, and many adolescent and adult criminal offenders" in the preconventional level; "most adolescents and adults in our society and in other societies" in the conventional level; and "a minority of adults... only after age 20" in the postconventional level.[13]

What motivates the individual to respond at a particular stage varies. Stage 1 involves the avoidance of punishment. It is pure obedience to avoid pain. Stage 2 is one of reciprocity or "social hedonism." Conformity occurs so that rewards can be obtained in return. There is a fair exchange wherein good behavior is repaid. Stage 3 is one of "good boy/ nice girl" morality. Rules are followed so as to gain approval of others and to avoid the disapproval of others. Stage 4 represents an "unthinking respect," an unquestioning adherence to authority, simply because a legitimate authority cannot be doubted. Stage 5 represents a "social contract" wherein rules are accepted democratically for the general welfare of all. Social harmony is maintained through mutual respect of the rights of others. Stage 6 represents a logical evaluation of rules. In this stage moral principles are self-accepted. Self-condemnation is avoided by a "let your conscience be your own guide" philosophy. Behavior is followed not "by convention," but "on principle."

With regard to motivation for each of the three major levels, the individual at the preconventional level has not yet begun to "understand" society's rules and expectations. The conventional-level person understands in his/her own way that he/she must adhere to the rules and expectations of society simply because these exist as having been promulgated by a legitimate authority or simply because these rules represent conventionality. Persons at the post-conventional level "understand" and even formulate the underlying moral principles that give rise to the rules and expectations. It should be noted that whether or not Kohlberg's sixth stage is as empirically based as are his first five, all six stages represent a schema for inclusion into discussion here.[14]

The Classical Conditioning Approach

Classical conditioning makes use of associative learning. In the experiments of Ivan Pavlov, a repeated pairing of food with a sound produced an association such that the sound eventually sufficed to evoke a reflexive response which the food normally calls forth.[15] Pavlov found that the dog would involuntarily respond by salivating upon the presentation of the stimulus (food). This is an "unconditioned response" to an "unconditioned stimulus," because food naturally produces an unlearned response of salivation in dogs. Pavlov repeatedly paired the food stimulus with a tone (bell or buzzer). The dog, of course, salivated at the presentation of food (paired with the tone). Afterwards, when the tone was presented alone (in the absence of the food), it was able to evoke the response of salivation. The new response is a "conditioned" or "learned" response to a "conditioned" stimulus. A previously neutral stimulus (the tone) was formerly incapable of evoking the natural, reflexive response of salivation. However, the dog had learned to associate the tone with the food.

In natural settings, one can find classical learning or associative learning to be taking place among individuals, sometimes in subtle ways. One form of such learning, "vicarious classical conditioning," can be seen as a learning of certain emotions or attitudes experienced by children through their parents. For instance, racial prejudice can be learned by children after their having heard the parent repeatedly pair a racial group with derogatory terms.[16] The previously neutral stimulus, e.g., a black person, is later encountered by the child. He/she associates his/her parents' feelings with the learned stimulus, and consequently responds in a negative manner toward the black person. It is conceivable that attitudes toward authorities, laws, conformity, etc., can be learned in similar fashion.

The Operant Conditioning Approach

Attitudes can be conditioned; however, the learning process that is involved categorically falls somewhere in between the processes of classical and operant conditioning.[17] Operant or "instrumental" conditioning involves voluntary, rather than reflexive, responses. In this process the individual (or animal) is rewarded or punished for what he/she does or for what he/she fails to do. The subject's responses are "reinforced" so as to increase desirable behavior and to decrease undesirable behavior. B. F. Skinner has done some major work in this area to help prove that "behavior is a consequence of environment."[18]

In the process of operant conditioning, the uncompleted desirable act is reinforced by the process of

29

"shaping." Accordingly, graduated approximations of the desired behavior are rewarded until the completed, desired behavior is produced (and, of course, rewarded if its repetition is desired). Operant conditioning serves to increase the rate of desired behavior and to decrease the rate of (or "extinguish") undesired behavior. The person in control of dispensing reinforcers presents or removes them contingent upon the presentation of behavior by the subject. The reinforcers can be pleasant or unpleasant (aversive). The chart in Table 4 illustrates the simple process of presenting or removing pleasant or unpleasant consequences.

TABLE 4

OPERANT CONDITIONING

	Presenting	Removing
Pleasant	I Positive Reinforcement	II Omission
Unpleasant	III Punishment	IV Negative Reinforcement

Box I represents an increase in desirable behavior upon the presentation of a pleasant reinforcer (a reward). Box II represents a decrease in undesirable behavior upon the removal of a pleasant reinforcer. Often this pleasant reinforcer has been operating unbeknownst to the controller of rewards and punishments. This is the case of the school teacher who does not realize that his/her chastising of an unruly student in front of other class members is actually serving as a positive reinforcer, because the student is receiving his/her desired attention. When the teacher realizes this, he/she can remove the attention. His/her action would then be a deliberate omission, resulting in a decrease in undesirable behavior. Box III also represents a decrease in undesirable behavior, but through presenting an unpleasant reinforcer contingent upon the display of an undesirable behavior. Box IV represents an increase in desirable behavior when an unpleasant reinforcer is removed. If the subject were receiving punishment, then the punishment could be removed contingent upon the presentation of the desired behavior.

"Behavior therapy," "behavior modification," and "aversion therapy" are present-day therapeutic devices for behavioral change.[19] These practices are concerned with systematic contingency management to bring about changes in overt behavior. These therapies do not attempt to change the values that underlie the behavior.

The Social Learning Approach

Albert Bandura recognized that with the advent of principles of reinforcement, theoretical explanations of learning began to focus on instrumental response acquisition based upon reinforcing outcomes.[20] Bandura conducted experiments on the effects of indirect and direct reinforcement. He also acknowledged an "observational learning," which is based merely on imitation of models. In observational learning, an individual acquires a novel behavior that had not yet been a part of his/her behavioral repertoire. The observer later reproduces the behavior when faced with appropriate stimuli. This is copying behavior, learned from observing a model. To reproduce the model's behavior does necessitate the observer's attention, memory, motivation, and physical ability to copy the particular behavior.

Indirect reinforcement is described by Bandura as a method of providing "inhibitory" and "disinhibitory" effects.[21] The learner witnesses the model's behavior and the consequences that befall the model. In turn, the learner is likely to imitate the behavior after having witnessed the model receive rewarding consequences. The learner is unlikely to imitate the behavior after having witnessed punishing consequences. Direct reinforcement is merely being the recipient of consequences, rather than witnessing another's receipt of consequences. An experiment of Bandura's combines indirect and direct reinforcement processes in the learning of aggressive behavior.[22] In the experiment, children were divided into three groups to witness a model displaying aggressiveness. One group saw the model receive punishment. Another group saw the model receive rewards. The third group saw no consequences come to the model. A test of imitation afterwards showed a greater variety of imitative behavior on the part of those children in the model-rewarded group, followed by the nonconsequences group, compared to the model-punished group. The next part of the experiment provided attractive incentives directly to the children (to be used as reinforcers after appropriate behavior display) with the children aware that they would receive these rewards for imitative behavior. The differences in imitative performance among the three groups disappeared, indicating that learning had taken place in all three groups.

While each of the above major perspectives of learning can stand alone, together they provide a comprehensive view of the myriad of experiences to which individuals are subjected during their everyday routine. The differences among the theories do, in fact, extend beyond the idiosyncrasies of their proponents. However, it may be unnecessary to take the term "socialization" and try to embellish it with all of the major perspectives in its definition. The writer is now able to operationally define socialization (and resocialization) here for the study's purposes.

Socialization Defined: The Relative Importance of Knowledge, Ability, and Motivation

Although theorists differ in their precise definitions of the term socialization, they do agree that it represents an ongoing learning process. Some, such as the stage theorists, will want to delineate sub-categories representing changes in the content of what is being learned. Others simply differ in their choice stressing particular areas of content that are being learned. If one refers back to Brim's discussion of socialization (see Table 2), accordingly, socialization would be defined as an ongoing learning process in which the novice gains the following:
  a.   knowledge of the group's expected behavior and values;
  b.   the ability to follow the group's expected behavior and values;
  c.   the motivation to pursue the group's expected behavior and values.

Resocialization can, therefore, be defined as a continuation of socialization to correct deficits in the individual's knowledge, ability, and motivation for the group's expected behavior and values. From the discussion of self-other theory, it would seem that significant others provide the knowledge to the novice. Reinforcement theory indicates that a system of rewards and punishments provides the motivation to the novice.

Cognitive-developmental theory seems to suggest that a majority of society's members respond conventionally in a role-interpretation situation. This constitutes their motivation, as opposed to acting "on principle." Still, others in the preconventional level are responding in a reinforcement-like situation, again displaying a motivation that is not based on principle. Ability is most appropriately addressed in cognitive-developmental theory, which views ability primarily in terms of intellectual growth. Other theorists, such as Alex Inkeles and M. Brewster Smith, deal more elaborately with an equivalent concept of ability--"competence."[23]

Because the concept of ability has been dealt with only slightly in the socialization theories presented thus far, its importance will be elaborated upon here. Inkeles has defined competence as:

the ability to attain and perform in three sets of statuses: Those which one's society will normally assign one, those in the repertoire of one's social system that one may reasonably aspire to, and those which one might reasonably invent or elaborate for oneself.[24]

The key words in Inkeles' definition are "normally" and "reasonably"; for these concepts suggest that expectations be commensurate with ability.

M. Brewster Smith traces the paths of "benign" and "vicious circles" that can develop according to the degree of competence held by an individual.[25] The benign circle depicts the person whose ability is matched with his/her environmental demands (and these do include social expectations). This individual's successes in coping will reinforce further efforts. Success is gratifying and promotes a favorable attitude for further learning and accomplishments. On the other hand, persons not as fortunate, who get off to a bad start, generate further failure and consequent negative attitudes toward society. This individual falls behind in his/her accomplishments and, in turn, falls behind in further attempts to succeed. In this circle, the individual is not acquiring the knowledge and the skills that are being acquired by his/her successful counterpart. It would seem that the component "motivation" is integrally related to and dependent upon the components "ability" and "knowledge." The product of a

33

benign circle becomes intrinsically motivated toward competence.

Brim considers the priorities which society arranges for knowledge, ability, and motivation of expected behavior and values. According to Brim, it is easier for society to assume that motivation is the source for deviance, rather than to assume that the cause is ignorance or lack of ability. A functional aspect of this assumption is that it places the blame on the individual, rather than on the society.

> If a person confronts his society with a claim of ignorance or poor ability, it reflects on the adequacy of his prior socialization, which is society's responsibility. Motivational deviance, in contrast, is less easily attributable to defects in society's socialization process and is more easily viewed as being the individual's own fault.[26]

Accordingly, society "pays the price" when we are engaged in resocialization.

> The treatment of deviance would be more effective if it made use of techniques which accord with the reasons for behavior: where ignorance is the cause, education; where lack of ability is the difficulty, improved training; where motivation is the problem, a planned and deliberately executed program of manipulation of rewards and punishments to reorient the individual to appropriate goals and behavior. . . . If deviance comes from ignorance or lack of ability and yet punishment is administered in the mistaken idea that motivation is the cause, a frequent result is the individual's rejection of the values of society which he formerly accepted.[27]

Another reason which one might posit for a societal assumption that motivation is the cause of deviance may be what social psychologists refer to as "attributional error."[28] When someone is the victim of an unfortunate mishap, e.g., physical injury in an auto accident, we tend to fortify our own feelings of safety by blaming the individual as the cause of his/her own mishap. In this way, we can feel assured that the same

34

type of incident is unlikely to happen to us. If we were to account for the accident in terms of external factors, e.g., faulty auto brakes, then there is a greater likelihood that the same type of accident could happen to us. It is suggested that through the process of "attributional error" (in this case, blaming the individual for lack of motivation), society can feel safe that the majority of its members will not depart from the norms. Motivation is viewed by society as an internal factor, achieved by the individual mostly through his/her own decision, whereas knowledge and ability are viewed as external in that they are conferred upon the individual by society through its educative efforts. The society is responsible for the individual's lack of knowledge and ability, whereas the individual is responsible for his/her own lack of motivation.

Internal Versus External Mechanisms of Control

With the above thought of accountability (individual versus environment) kept in mind, attention can now be directed to the dichotomy of internal and external mechanisms of social control. Separating models of socialization into categories of internal and external mechanisms can serve to accentuate, and thereby identify, the model which the probation-supervision process relies upon. The probation-supervision process is making use of several of the models, while relying heavily upon the practical application of primarily one of the models.

The preceding discussion of attributional error concluded with the thought that motivation is an internal quality achieved by the individual, while knowledge and ability are external factors bestowed upon the individual by the society. The question arises as to which theories of socialization view the individual as a passive recipient of his/her culture. The alternative question remains as to which of the theories view the individual as an active decision-maker, choosing to conform to his/her culture, or choosing to deviate from it.

The psychoanalytic theory would appear to be emphasizing internal mechanisms. Initially the individual has no control over his/her id. When the time is appropriate for the formation of the superego, its development is dependent mainly upon the individual's choice. Society provides the standards for perfection;

but it is the individual who must internalize these. If the standards are internalized, then the conscience is formed, providing the individual with a mechanism of self-control. With regard to Erikson's developmental theory, the method of control is shared somewhat with others. The outcome of each crisis period is determined by the reactions that others display toward novel acts of the individual. The individual subconsciously becomes influenced in his/her attitudes about himself/herself and others through the reactions of those around him/her. The subconscious, internal control outweighs all other factors contributing to the individual's behavior.

The self-other theories are theories of "interactionism," connoting a balance of control between the individual and his/her environment. However, it appears that the individual responds to feedback from others, rather than others adhering to the expectations of the individual. For this reason, the referent, or point of control, involved in self-other theories may be said to be more external than internal.

The cognitive-developmental theories place emphasis on the readiness of the individual to hold abstract thought. The intellectual preparation is a prerequisite to moral maturation. According to Kohlberg, the preconventional level of morality is characterized by external means of control (avoidance of punishment, and by social exchange). The conventional level is characterized by external rules and the social approval of others. It is not until the postconventional level (which a minority of Americans reach) that the individual is on his/her own, logically evaluating and formulating rules. The majority of us have not reached the third level, but are in the second level. Most of us, therefore, never experience the internal mechanism of control or we reach it after first experiencing two external levels of control that dominate our early years (before age 20). Under these circumstances, cognitive-developmental theory would be supportive of an external mechanism of control for most persons and an internal mechanism of control for some.

Classical conditioning involves reflexes or involuntary responses. This factor precludes internal control. However, in the present usage of the term "vicarious classical conditioning" examples are provided which deal with emotions that are not reflexes. Nonetheless, even with the substitution of emotions for reflexes, the individual's learning experience in classical conditioning is being provided by someone other than the individual. Someone else arranges the association or pairing to be learned. Classical conditioning, therefore, represents an external mechanism of control.

Operant conditioning is based exclusively on an external mechanism of control. A behavior may be shaped or it may appear on its own. The increase or decrease in the behavior is dependent upon administered rewards and punishments. It is true that human beings are using thought processes that allow information processing to take place during this type of conditioning. Lower animals are reacting to the systematic reinforcement without the mediating thought processes that are unique to human beings. Nonetheless, the individual's thoughts (and, therefore, actions) are dependent upon the external mechanism of environmental consequences.

Social learning theory is also based upon an external frame of reference. Models provide cues for the copying of their behavior. Even in mere observational learning, the attributes of the model can influence whether or not his/her behavior will be imitated (e.g., similarity of the model to the observer). A more pronounced influence upon the observer occurs during indirect reinforcement, where rewards and punishments toward models are witnessed. Direct reinforcement is an equivalent of operant conditioning. All three of these forms of social learning represent an external mechanism of control.

Figure 1 illustrates the degree of internal or external reference held for each of the aforementioned major theories:

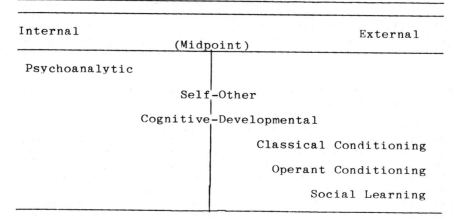

Internal	(Midpoint)	External
Psychoanalytic		
	Self-Other	
	Cognitive-Developmental	
		Classical Conditioning
		Operant Conditioning
		Social Learning

Figure 1. Internal versus external mechanism of control.

The Probation-Supervision Process and Its Use of Control

Chapter III will present the probation-supervision process as a model. The elements of the model will be identified according to the priorities that appear to be operating in the probation-supervision system. One of those elements can be introduced here--mechanism of control. While the probation-supervision process makes use of several of the aforementioned models, it relies greatly upon operant conditioning, or more precisely, reinforcement. The probation-supervision process contrives explicit contingencies, known in advance to the probationer, and applies rewards and punishments based on obedience to its demands. There is little or no concern about whether the underlying values for the desired behavior will be internalized. For this reason, when the probation-supervision process model addresses itself to its method, the concept of external mechanism of control will be included. Because the outcome of the probation-supervision process is dependent upon the method employed, the model of the process will show a very superficial type of learning taking place.

It is noteworthy that Walter C. Reckless has dealt with the concepts of "internal containment" and "external containment" in his theory of the individual's bout with the pressures and pulls fostering criminality.[29] According to Reckless, there is an external layer of containment encircling the individual to help dissuade him/her from criminal acts. Groups in the individual's normative environment comprise the layer of external containment. Reckless refers to the group's influence upon the tempted and/or frustrated would-be criminal as "outer containment." Reckless identifies a distant layer of containment within the individual, stemming from his/her successful or unsuccessful norm internalization, ego strength, self-control, self-concept, etc. This layer is referred to as "inner containment."

Harjit S. Sandhu has found an application of Reckless' containment theory for the treatment of incarcerated offenders.[30] Sandhu is able to classify treatment facilities (e.g., minimum security, medium security, and maximum security) according to the individual's inner and outer containment strengths.

While it is recognized that the probation-supervision process can vary its method with regard to intensive treatment plans, such plans are usually experimental or for other reasons short-lived. Primarily, probation-supervision operates through an external mechanism of control for faulty containment, without distinguishing between inner and outer containment.

Notes

[1] See Allen Pincus and Anne Minahan, <u>Social Work Practice: Model and Method</u> (Itasca, Ill.: F. E. Peacock Publishing Co., 1973) wherein these authors distinguish between the "client" and the "potential client." The "potential client" can be identified as someone in need of services, but not requesting the help. The practitioner can direct his/her efforts in such a way that a "potential client" becomes the recipient of the needed service, without having initiated the request.

[2] The reader will note that a select few theorists have been chosen, to the exclusion of other, more recent contributors. This is not a "review of the literature" on socialization.

[3] See Chapter I for information regarding the specific works of each of these theorists.

[4] Sigmund Freud, <u>An Outline of Psychoanalysis</u>, trans. J. Strachey (New York: Norton, 1949).

[5] <u>Ibid.</u>

[6] Erikson, pp. 247-74.

[7] Stage 5 is associated with the period of adolescence; Stage 6, young adulthood; Stage 7, young adulthood and middle age; and Stage 8, old age.

[8] Cooley; Mead.

[9] First stated by Edwin H. Sutherland, and later expanded upon in collaboration with his student, Donald R. Cressey, the refined formulation of the theory of "differential association" can be found in Edwin H. Sutherland and Donald R. Cressey, <u>Criminology</u>, 10th ed. (Philadelphia: J. B. Lippincott Co., 1978), pp. 80-83. According to Sutherland's thesis, the persons with whom an individual systematically interacts foster definitions that are either favorable or unfavorable to crime. The comparison to Mead's concept of "significant others" is not a complete one. Mead's significant others are not sought out by the individual in the way that Sutherland's role models are. Further, Mead's significant others have more than just psychic influence and technical knowledge to impart to the novice. Mead's significant others have some control over "rewards" and "punishments."

[10]Jean Piaget, The Origins of Intelligence in Children, trans. M. Cook (New York: International Universities Press, 1969).

[11]Kohlberg, p. 32.

[12]Ibid., pp. 33-35.

[13]Ibid., p. 33.

[14]Howard Muson, "Moral Thinking: Can It Be Taught?" Psychology Today (February, 1979): 57.

[15]Ivan P. Pavlov, Conditioned Reflexes (New York: Macmillan, 1927).

[16]See Robert A. Baron and Donn Byrne, Social Psychology: Understanding Human Interaction 3rd ed. (Boston: Allyn & Bacon, 1981), pp. 93-95. These authors speak of the acquisition of strong irrational fears (e.g., phobias of certain animals) and the development of intense racial or ethnic prejudices as the product of vicarious classical conditioning.

[17]Brian Sutton-Smith, Child Psychology (New York: Appleton-Century-Crofts, 1973), p. 34.

[18]B. F. Skinner, Science and Human Behavior (New York: Macmillan, 1953).

[19]Bandura, 1969; Roland G. Tharp and Ralph J. Wetzel, Behavior Modification in the Natural Environment (New York: Academic Press, 1969).

[20]Bandura, p. 121. See also Albert Bandura and Richard Walters, Social Learning and Personality Development (New York: Holt, Rinehart & Winston, 1963).

[21]Bandura, p. 120.

[22]Albert Bandura, "Influence of models' reinforcement contingencies on the acquisition of imitative responses," Journal of Personality and Social Psychology 1 (1965): 589-95.

[23]Alex Inkeles, "Social Structure and the Socialization of Competence," Harvard Educational Review 36 (1963): 265-83; M. Brewster Smith, "Competence and Socialization," in Socialization and Society, ed. John A. Clausen (Boston: Little, Brown & Co., 1968), pp. 272-320.

[24]Inkeles is quoted by Smith, p. 274.

[25]Ibid., pp. 276-77.

[26]Brim, p. 43.

[27]Ibid.

[28]For further discussion of "attributional error" and its consequent "defensive attribution of responsibility," see Robert A. Baron and Donn Byrne, Exploring Social Psychology (Boston: Allyn & Bacon, 1979), pp. 47-49.

[29]Walter C. Reckless, The Crime Problem (New York: Appleton-Century-Crofts, 1961), pp. 355-56.

[30]Harjit S. Sandhu, Modern Corrections (Springfield, Ill.: Charles C. Thomas Publishing Co., 1974), p. 37.

Chapter III

THE PROBATION-SUPERVISION PROCESS AS A MODEL

Reliance on External Mechanisms of Control

In Chapter II, it was found that socialization can be viewed as a process relying heavily on either internal mechanisms or external mechanisms, or relying on neither of the extremes (see figure 1). It appears that the probation-supervision process (hereafter referred to as the P-S process) relies heavily on external mechanisms in its method to resocialize. This is consistent with the view that, if internal mechanisms have failed in the socialization process, it is easier to work with external means rather than to belabor the failing internal means to correct the situation. Another factor in the reliance on external mechanisms by the P-S process is simply the appropriateness of that type of control for a secondary-group, disaffective process.

Specifically, the P-S process makes the greatest use of reinforcement theory. The authoritative, even threatening, framework in which probation officers function allows them to implement a system of behavior modification. The probation officer does not have to search for some of the reinforcers. These are already built into the P-S process. Positive reinforcers include a successful, administrative termination of probation and an early, successful termination of probation. Negative reinforcers include a violation of probation (which could result in a revocation of probation supervision, followed by a resentencing, or could result in an extension of probation). The persons in a position to apply the reinforcers, contingent upon the appropriate response from the probationer, are the probation officer and, through him/her, the court judge. Table 5 illustrates some of the contingencies which could be set up by the P-S process.

TABLE 5

REINFORCEMENT CONTINGENCIES IN THE P-S PROCESS

	Presenting	Removing
Pleasant Stimulus	I Notification of Administrative Termination of P-S	II Court Revocation of P-S
Unpleasant Stimulus	III Filing a Violation of P-S	IV Early Successful Termination of P-S

While the probationer may not enjoy being under probation supervision, he/she, nonetheless, does not want to "lose" that status through a violation of probation proceedings. When the status is revoked, the case could result in a resentencing to incarceration. While he/she does not want to lose the status, the probationer would prefer that the status be successfully terminated, either when his/her case is administratively scheduled to close or, even better, earlier than the case's scheduled termination. The reader will note that boxes I and IV of Table 5 share the same use of a reinforcer--the termination of probation supervision. Box I represents the probationer's "receipt" of a letter of notification which advises him/her that he/she has completed his/her commitment. The same letter contains a clause: "Thank you for your cooperation." The receipt of the letter is tantamount to having been told that the P-S process is certifying a successful graduate from its program. In this use of the probation-supervision status, it is true that one is actually also "removing" an "unpleasant stimulus" in box I. However, it may be more appropriate to highlight the fact that one is "presenting" a "pleasant stimulus"--a new status of earned freedom to the probationer. In box IV, the closing of the case has occurred earlier than originally scheduled. Box IV, therefore, represents a gesture of "relieving" the probationer of his/

44

her probationer status, and thereby "granting" him/her freedom earlier than had been intended. This "granting" of freedom can be seen also as "presenting" a "pleasant stimulus." For this reason, boxes 1 and IV become only distinguishable through a "matter of semantics" concerning the terms "removing" and "presenting." The other factor that distinguishes boxes I and IV from each other is the time element of when probation supervision terminates. It should be noted that box III (filing a violation of probation) could lead to box II (court revocation of probation supervision). Thus, presenting an unpleasant stimulus (box III) may be a means toward a goal of removing a pleasant stimulus (box II).

Thus far, it has been established that the P-S process model employs as a method the reliance on external, rather than internal, mechanisms of control. Other aspects of the P-S process model and its method can now be discussed. It is the author's proposal that the P-S process must rely upon observable, "opportunistic" behavior accomplished through an obedience relationship. These aspects of method will be dealt with separately here.

Observable Behavior versus "Nonobservable Nonbehavior"

Thoughts, feelings, and moods are internal states with which the probation officer is concerned. However, internal states are "nonobservable nonbehaviors." The phrase nonobservable nonbehaviors emphasizes that attitudes are privately held. It is recognized that there is considerable belief in the accuracy involved in measuring attitudes through surveys, as well as through indirect (projective) methods. However, internal states are known only to the holder unless they become transformed into overt action or observable behavior. Even observable behavior can be misperceived and, more importantly, misinterpreted. Howard S. Becker's concept of the "falsely accused" illustrates a societal (or group) failure to perceive correctly the behavior of the nondeviant.[1] An individual can be performing in accordance with normative standards and yet society can "see" deviance where there is none.

Table 6 represents Becker's varieties of perceptions of deviance. Boxes II and III indicate societal failure to perceive deviant behavior accurately. In box II, society mistakenly believes that someone is performing deviantly. In box III, deviance is occurring covertly, unbeknownst to society.

45

TABLE 6

THE PERCEPTION OF DEVIANCE

Societal Perception	Actual Behavior	
	Rule Breaking	Rule Abiding
Rule Breaking	I Pure Deviant	II Falsely Accused
Rule Abiding	III Secret Deviant	IV Conformist

Selectivity is sometimes the cause of inaccurate perception. A classic study by Gordon Allport and Leo Postman illustrates the human potential for selective perception.[2] In the particular study cited, subjects are shown a scene in which a menacing, white male is holding an open razor and arguing with a timid-appearing black male. Subjects later reported having seen the razor in the hand of the black male. In non-experimental conditions, persons (especially highly conventional types) are susceptible to seeing mostly what they want to see or what they expect to see.

Misinterpretation of behavior can be a function of the actor, as well as a function of the viewer. The actor can purposely deceive the viewer by acting contrary to the actor's true beliefs. In this case the actor may harbor tendencies for deviant behavior and, while he/she may act out these tendencies on other occasions, he/she may purposely act out superficial normative behavior when he/she knows that he/she is being observed. Becker would refer to this individual as the "secret deviant." Both the "falsely accused" and the "secret deviant" represent societal misinterpretation, as well as misperception. Putting aside the case of the actor misleading the viewer, the fact remains that it is difficult in itself to accurately attribute internal states to an individual's actions.

There is the alternative case wherein the observer assumes insincerity in attitude change. When

he/she sees failure in behavioral change, he/she assumes that the individual never intended to succeed.
In this instance, the actor promised behavioral change
and may have experienced attitudinal change; but social
forces may have impinged upon the individual's expression of the behavior. David Matza's concept of "soft
determinism" suggests that the individual is neither
completely governed by free will, nor is he/she completely governed by determinism.[3] Whenever one views a
relapse of a lawbreaker, one ought to consider the possibility that some force outside the individual's
complete control may have contributed to a failure in
manifesting behavior which the individual had intended
to display. The most serious failing on society's part
is to let the individual know that we have no faith in
a stated promise of behavioral change. In doing so, we
may abort the change through a self-fulfilling prophecy. It is true that probation officers, after a number
of years on the job, can come to think of themselves as
seasoned in detecting lies. However, when probation
officers become predictors of their clients' promises,
they begin to resemble Jerome Skolnick's police officer
who, when making an arrest, tries and convicts his/her
suspects on the spot.[4]

Social psychologists remain engrossed in investigating the process of "attribution" or inferring the
motives, intentions, and stable dispositions of others
through observing their overt behavior and appearance.[5] Inasmuch as it is difficult to accurately know
internal states through mere observation, we must rely
upon psychological testing, e.g., personality invento-
ries, projective tests, etc. These are rarely available to the probation officer. There is no routine
diagnostic process applied by the Metropolitan Area
Department of Probation nor by its court system. A
court psychiatrist may be asked to examine and diag-
nose. However, such examinations are not performed in
depth. Occasionally, these tests are available through
a probationer's prior contact with another agency or
with a private psychiatrist or psychologist. In the
absence of such information, the probation officer must
rely upon interview data of his/her own and past records of behavior, as well as current perceptions (or
misperceptions) of behavior.

Given the above limitations, the P-S process must
focus on observable behavior as the target for change.
Such behavior is subject, of course, to inaccurate perception and interpretation. The P-S process is faced

47

with the task of bringing about behavioral change which, in turn, is hoped to lead to attitudinal change. While evidence exists for the notion that attitudinal changes may lead to behavioral changes, probation officers must focus their attention on the opposite transition--behavioral changes bringing about attitudinal changes. This latter transition is also supported by the literature.[6]

"Opportunistic Learning" versus "Propriate Learning"

While all normal individuals are capable of learning behavior through reinforcement, not everyone is capable of learning the supporting values to the extent that such values become internalized. Gordon Allport has distinguished between the two forms of learning and has illustrated the sociopath as a type capable of opportunistic learning and incapable of propriate learning.[7] According to Allport, the sociopath can perform normative behavior without any concomitant value intake. Others may do the same during very early stages of development; however, when cognitive capacities permit, these individuals go beyond the process of contingency management to develop a set of intrinsic societal values. The sociopath will be discussed later as one criminal type who is incapable of internalizing societal values as his/her own. However, it should be recognized that virtually everyone is potentially capable of being fixated at the stage of opportunistic learning. Kohlberg's stages of preconventional morality encompass much behavior of so-called "normal" individuals, e.g., nonsociopaths. Yet persons who occupy the stage of preconventional morality have not progressed beyond opportunistic learning.

Given the above, it may be safe to say that we operate within a caveat wherein nonobservable nonbehaviors may exist contrary to an individual's observable behavior; and an individual's observable behavior may reflect only a primitive accomplishment confined to hedonism in the absence of authentic commitment to norms. The probation officer, therefore, is working with these constraints. It may be that we have no way of measuring the authenticity of norm commitment for any individual. Therefore, if the P-S process operates to insure conformity to norms, there will be no accurate method to gauge the accompanying internal state. Measures can only pertain to the observable behavior which comes about through "obedience."

48

"Conformity," "Compliance," and "Obedience"

Social psychologists distinguish each of the following three terms from the other: "conformity," "compliance," and "obedience."[8] All three are the result of social influence; however, each is characterized by its own relationship between the actor and the group to which he/she is responding. "Conformity" will be thought of here as behavior resulting from the actor's implicit assumptions about approval and disapproval from others. Solomon Asch and Muzafer Sherif, in their respective works, have demonstrated the preoccupation that individuals can have predisposing them to act similar to others so as not to be looked upon disfavorably.[9] The pressure to act in a certain way stems from the individual's own perception of anticipatory acceptance or rejection by others. Nothing has been explicitly put to the individual by the group to insure the conformity. Our social strivings are interdependent upon conformity or acting similar to others for acceptance.

"Compliance," however, is resulting behavior corresponding to an explicit request by another individual (or group of individuals). The group, or someone acting on their behalf, directly influences compliance by establishing a request. Whether it is a rule that one is being asked to comply with or whether it is simply a favor that one is being asked to perform, the explicitness is there. There is usually an expressed future counterbehavior. For instance, rules and regulations usually carry with them a statement of the consequences one faces for an infraction (for noncompliance). In the case of an individual requesting a favor, there may be an explicit statement on his/her part that he/she will return the favor in the future. In other cases, the individual is faced with only the request and not the direct expression of a future returned or counterbehavior. In these instances, the actor can anticipate the counterbehavior based upon factors dealing with the nature of his/her relationship to the person making the request. One anticipation might be the loss of the existing relationship (friend to friend, employee to employer, etc.) between the two.

The third and last category of social influence is "obedience," which resembles "compliance" in that both involve explicit, direct pressure. The degree of pressure is stronger in the "obedience" relationship. Here the group (or individual representing the group) makes more than a request. A command is given which is supported by explicit repercussions if there is a failure to obey on the part of the actor. There is an expressed ultimatum provided in the obedience relationship based upon the status held by the individual making the command and, most importantly, based upon the power that this individual has to carry out the reprisals for disobedience.

The P-S process constitutes an atmosphere for both compliance and obedience relationships, with the emphasis being on obedience. Norm adherence by a probationer would not constitute conformity in the present use of this term. We can assume no concomitant commitment to norms simply on the basis of our witnessing socially approved behavior on the part of a probationer. He/she may only be responding at the level of pre-conventional morality where moral actions take place because of extraneous punishments and rewards.

It has been suggested here that the evaluation of probation supervision as a change agent rests on evidence of behavioral change only, since it is unlikely that probation officers can know whether attitudinal change has taken place. The methods which probation supervision implements constitute a system of behavior modification wherein the probation officer/probationer dyad is based primarily upon the influence of obedience (not conformity). However, the combination of external mechanisms of control, reliance upon observable behavior, and an obedience relationship may conceivably lead to only opportunistic learning.

The P-S Process Formulated

For the remaining elements of the P-S process model, it is necessary to turn to Brim's model of adult socialization and then to Kennedy and Kerber's model of resocialization. Both of these models can be modified somewhat to incorporate them into the P-S process model.

As previously mentioned in Chapter I, Brim's model proposes that society places its priority on knowledge of expected behavior when society is considering adult socialization. It would seem that the P-S process can work only within the tangible category, "behavior," and not within the abstract category of values. Further, true "motivation" experienced by the probationer seems to be beyond the probation officer's scope. Therefore, cells E and F (Table 2) are virtually eliminated from the P-S process model. The only supposed motivation for behavior which one is able to conjecture is judged by cell A, demonstrated knowledge of expected behavior. Cell B, knowledge of expected values, cannot be included in the model, because propriate learning and internal mechanisms of control have already been eliminated. Cells C and D refer to ability to pursue expected behavior and values. The P-S process allows for very little thought to be given to ability. The probation officer assumes that the ability is present and will be used to pursue the expected behavior if the proper contingencies are contrived. The ability to pursue the values is also assumed to be present, but unobservable. If one chooses to think of "ability" as the possession of skills and education, then one does find some concern shown by probation officers when probationers are referred for educational and job training programs. However, in reality, the prospects for our nation's job training programs are dismal. Waiting lists are discouraging, funding is low, and the reputation of federal programs for saturating the job market with too many people possessing the same skill is known. Probation officers may go through the motions of being a resource system to the probationer, e.g., apprising him/her of the availability of programs, initiating a referral, etc.; however, that is where the process stops. The success rate for actually linking the probationer with a skill is virtually nil.

Modification of Brim's model appears in Table 7. Cell E is selected instead of cell A for priority. This selection is made because reinforcement is actually concentrating on motivational forces. However, as previously mentioned, motivation itself is not an element conducive to the observational measurements upon which the P-S process rests. The actual modification that has been made to Brim's model is that cell A has been highlighted to represent opportunistic, rather than propriate, knowledge. Therefore, the P-S process model gives priority to motivation for expected behavior. Knowledge of expected behavior is recognized to be of an opportunistic nature only. (See the revision of Brim's model in Table 7).

With regard to Kennedy and Kerber's model, each of their twelve identifiers (for the individual and for the agent during resocialization) can be incorporated into the P-S process model. The first of these identi-

fiers is the individual's "accumulated experiences."
It will be seen that those persons processed through
probation supervision come into the system with accumulated experiences that are contrary to approved societal behavior. These experiences naturally began within the family unit, the first primary-group experience.
The peer group served as another primary-group experience, while the school (as a secondary-group experience) gave the individual still new perspectives in the
learning process. The school experience serves to extend the learning of norms to a more pragmatic setting
than the family experience is able to do. The "traditional" classroom helps to foster the norms of achievement, independence, universalism, and specificity.[10]
Adherence to the norm of achievement results in the al-
location of individuals to future positions within the
school system and within the larger society. At times,
a lower-class subculture will form in retaliation to
the school's imposition of middle-class standards.[11]
This is an old theme, which is, nonetheless, still relevant today. Independence is fostered in the traditional classroom by instruction to work separately, not
collaboratively during exams, etc. Universalism and
specificity are fostered by the traditional classroom's
treatment of age-cohorts equally as members of a category based exclusively on the attribute of age. There
is no room for particularistic treatment in the traditional classroom the way in which such treatment had
been found by the child in the family setting. For
this reason, it is said that the secondary-group experience of the school serves to extend the learning of
norms to a more pragmatic setting than the family is
able to do. The peer group, on the other hand, rein-
forces much of what had been learned in the family setting by allowing particularistic and diffused treatment, by allowing joint efforts, and by allowing alternative methods of achievement.

In any event, the school system is probably the
first secondary-group experience encountered by the individual. If it bears some organizational resemblances
to the P-S process, then Kennedy and Kerber's second
identifier (the agent's "secondary-group" appearance)
is appropriately matched with the individual's accumulated experiences. The P-S process is characterized by
secondary-group relations, even though it is a one-to-
one relationship between the probation officer and the
probationer. The nature of the relationship is impersonal and based upon universalism and specificity. The
probationer is treated as one of a category of law-

breakers, although some individual allowances for differential treatment are inevitably made by the probation officer when he/she, for example, recognizes a "situational criminal."[12] Further, when there are grounds for a violation of probation, the probation officer can use discretion and perhaps decide not to file the violation, based on particularistic treatment of the individual. Because such instances are very isolated, it is more often the case that universalistic considerations lead the probation officer to automatically file the violation of probation and even justify his/her action to the probationer by explaining that the matter had been "out of his/her hands." This opportunity is always available in the P-S process which can hold the probationer accountable for any circumstances that befall him/her. The "Beccarian" insinuation is that the outcome (reaction) of the P-S process rests entirely upon the actions of the probationer himself/herself.[13] Like other behavior modification systems, the P-S process is an action-reaction system, with the probationer always initiating the behavior, and the probation officer always responding. The reaction of the probation officer serves to reinforce the behavior of the probationer.

The direct process of changing another's behavior is labelled by Kennedy and Kerber's third identifier as an expected outcome on the part of the individual to "alter" in response to the fourth identifier, an effort on the part of the agent to "redirect." It is the job of the probation officer to help redirect antisocial behavior into law-abiding behavior. Previous systems had been responsible for guiding the direction of the individual's development. However, when these systems failed, the behavior which brought the individual to the attention of the court was shown to have been established instead. It is entirely possible that the socializers within the family actually intended to teach antisocial behavior, and succeeded. Therefore, the demonstrated behavior which brings the individual to the court's attention may very well have been the product of a successful socialization into a deviant subculture. This is evident in the case of peer-group socialization, but should not be confined to that agent alone. The P-S process usually tries to distinguish between (a) whether the individual failed to respond to efforts on the part of the family to socialize him/her into the societal normative pattern, or (b) whether the family succeeded in socializing the individual into a deviant normative pattern. If the source of the antisocial behavior is identified, the P-S process has very little opportunity to work with the source. In this respect, the P-S process can be seen as failing to make use of the psychoanalytic method. The diffused intervention (probation supervision through the use of other agencies) may allow for a psychoanalytic therapy involvement for the probationer. However, such an involvement is problematic. If therapy occurs, it is not a component of the P-S process, but is a collateral system of its own.

The P-S process is primarily governed by reinforcement theory with a strict reliance on contingency management. The concept of social influence is relevant here in order to discuss Kennedy and Kerber's fifth, sixth, seventh, and eighth identifiers. The fifth and sixth identifiers view the individual as "independent" during the "disaffective" contact from the agent. The seventh and eighth identifiers view the individual as having to "comply" with the agent's efforts to "restore equilibrium." Again, it must be stressed that the P-S process is authority-based compliance or, more specifically, an obedience relationship. The court enforces the probation officer's commands, as these are in fact the court's commands verbalized by the probation officer. The probationer willingly (but through coercion) submits himself/herself to the commands of the probation officer and generally knows the consequences of a violation of the commands. The process is primarily a disaffective relationship, characterized by impersonal, aloof contacts. The probation officer does not "get involved" with the probationer's problem, but treats it objectively. However, there is some room for particularistic treatment, e.g., discretion, exceptions made due to mitigating circumstances, etc. Therefore, the P-S process may be labelled a secondary-group relationship because of its impersonality. It may also be said to have an element within it that is normally associated with primary groups—particularism.

Kennedy and Kerber's view of the individual as "independent," rather than dependent, needs further clarification (which is absent from their work). In the absence of such clarification, independence shall be interpreted to mean self-reliance while one is involved in the learning process. Dependence during the learning process would then characterize the initial period of socialization. This distinction appears problematic. There are situations in the P-S process

54

wherein the individual is inevitably "dependent" upon the probation officer for redirection, for approval of behavior, for maintenance of rewards, etc. It would appear that the behavior modification scheme calls for a dependent subject. Otherwise, the contingencies that the agent arranges would carry no strength.

Kennedy and Kerber's eighth identifier views the purpose of the resocialization process as "restoring equilibrium." The P-S process is attempting to initiate relearning. This effort entails unlearning before relearning.[14] This is most definitely an attempt to restore uniformity.

While Kennedy and Kerber use the term "comply" (as their seventh identifier), this term must be taken a step further in the P-S process--to "obey." The term "obey" is preferred, because there is power behind the probation officer to enforce directions.

The ninth, tenth, eleventh, and twelfth identifiers remain in accordance with the P-S model, with only a slight modification of the term "sporadic" (used by Kennedy and Kerber for the ninth and tenth identifiers). The P-S process does entail a noncontinuous contact. However, the atmosphere of the P-S process includes contact on a regular basis, e.g., reporting every three weeks, etc. In addition to the regularity of meetings between the probation officer and probationer, the system of contact is on a continuous schedule, rather than on an intermittent one. Considering the fault found with the term "sporadic," it is changed for the P-S process to "systematic."

There is no change to the eleventh and twelfth identifiers which characterize the setting of resocialization as being "artificial." The P-S process does operate in an artificial setting and that description is consistent with most secondary-group resocialization settings.

The revised models of Brim and of Kennedy and Kerber appear in Tables 7 and 8, respectively. The formulated P-S process model appears in Table 9.

TABLE 7

COMPARISON I

Brim: Adult Socialization

	Behavior		Values
Knowledge	Priority	A	B
Ability		C	D
Motivation		E	F

P-S Process:

	Behavior		Values
Knowledge	Opportunistic Learning	A	B Little Priority
Ability	Little Priority	C	D Little Priority
Motivation	Priority Nonobservable Nonbehavior	E	F Nonobservable Nonbehavior

TABLE 8

COMPARISON II

Kennedy and Kerber: Resocialization:

	Self	Agent
Who	Accumulated Experiences	Secondary Group
What	Alter	Redirect
How	Independent	Disaffective
Why	Comply	Restore Equilibrium
When	Sporadic	Sporadic
Where	Artificial Setting	Artificial Setting

P-S Process:

	Self	Agent
Who	Accumulated Experiences	Secondary-group Objectivity Primary-group One-to-one Relations
What	Alter	Redirect
How	Dependent	Disaffective with Particular Allowance
Why	Obey	Restore Equilibrium
When	Systematic	Systematic
Where	Artificial Setting	Artificial Setting

TABLE 9

THE P-S PROCESS FORMULATED

Priority	1.	Reformative
	2.	Demonstrated Knowledge of and Motivation for Expected Behavior
	3.	Ability is Given Little Priority or is Assumed
	4.	Values are Given No Priority but are Nonobservable Nonbehaviors
Method	1.	External Mechanism of Control
	2.	Reinforcement
	3.	Authority/Obedience
	4.	Secondary-Group Relations with an Element of Particularism
Outcome	1.	Opportunistic Learning

A Note on Organizational Factors in the P-S Process Model

Although organizational constraints of the P-S process will not be included in the model, a brief discussion of organizational factors is appropriate here. The case histories (which appear in Chapter IV) will illustrate the structural elements of the P-S process that may have some bearing on the efficiency of the re-socializing agent. Case history presentence investigations will be presented for the purpose of showing the preliminary task of probation officers that takes place before supervision can begin. The information accumulated during the probation-presentence investigation could prove to be decisive in formulating a proper plan for supervision. The amount of information and the quality of the information is not always consistent from one probation officer to another. Further, the same probation officer might prepare reports that differ from one another in terms of substance. An optimum (though not thorough) plan would be to have the investigating probation officer continue as the supervision probation officer. This had been done in the experimental, multi-functional branch in which this writer had worked. Even with this ideal condition, other

rules and regulations, staff apathy, etc., hampered the
P-S process from meeting its stated goals.

The writer did not see administrators initiate
changes to overcome structural shortcomings of the P-S
process. Administrators are viewed by the organization
as pace setters. If the administrators do not care
about the quality of the reports, then administrators
serve as models to the probation officers.[15] Caseload
size is one index to use in assessing whether the administrators favor quantity over quality in casework.
There are standards (set by the state) for caseload
size. However, these have been ignored by administrators in the Metropolitan Area Department of Probation.
When caseloads double the maximum limits, as was the
situation in Metropolitan Area, it can be seen that
volume is more important to the administrators than is
the quality of effort put forth by the probation officer. Under such conditions, there is little, if any,
opportunity or time available for quality in work.
Perhaps the probation officer models the same limited
effort to the probationer that has been modeled by the
administrators to the probation officer.

There remains another area of organization that
is of concern. Again, the onus is on administrators in
this instance. More detailed guidelines are needed
than already exist in Metropolitan Area's system that
explicitly ask for the inclusion of certain information
in reports. Guidelines should exist (and adherence to
them monitored) to require detailed statements about
home life (intact/other); siblings (ages, adjustment);
school (history, attitude toward); employment history;
prior arrests (dates, charges, outcomes, versions);
etc. Administrators had been responsible for insti-
tuting Metropolitan Area's "short-form" presentence investigation, which asks for less detail than previous
forms. This changeover may have been practical in
terms of saving time, but impractical in terms of
gathering information.

Organizational shortcomings of the P-S process no
doubt have an impact on the outcome of the process.
Case histories presented in Chapter IV must be read
with the above in mind. The reader will recognize that
there were opportunities in some of the case histories
for the P-S process to work closely with the probationer's family and/or peers (e.g., other participants
in the probationer's residential drug program). Yet
these opportunities were ignored. One can excuse the

failure to utilize family and peers in the reformative process only partially by categorizing the situation as caused by "organizational constraints," e.g., time limitations due to large caseloads, the failure of administrators to encourage innovative methods of treatment, etc. However, there was room for the probation officer's initiative to seek out the available persons to aid in the reformative process. One can only conjecture that probation officers (including this writer) were too engrossed in the use of the reinforcement method. Therefore, opportunities were ignored to supplement the dominant method of control with the other methods of socialization that were referred to in Chapter II. The case histories are provided to the reader for illustrations of the P-S process. It is difficult to find a meaningful amount of interaction between the probation officer and the probationers in these case histories. One reason for the scanty references to the interaction is that case records contained only short statements of the contacts. (Record keeping was conducted in a rushed, abbreviated manner.) These conditions were unavoidable due to excessive caseload size. When the ideal caseload size for Metropolitan Area had been set at 60, this writer had a caseload of more than 120.

The depth of the interactions with probationers was poor because of conditions that were beyond the probation officer's control. It is not the purpose here to expose deplorable work conditions that had been experienced in Metropolitan Area's Department of Probation. The adverse working conditions are mentioned in order to prepare the reader for the scarcity of information concerning contacts between the probation officer and probationers (that will be evident in the case histories). When the reader searches in vain for details of encounters in the case histories, the reader is actually finding an unnamed detail in the case histories--the brevity in interactions between probation officer and probationer. This is recognized as an element belonging to the P-S process; however, in the P-S process model, dysfunctional aspects of the formal organization are not included. The P-S process model includes only the manifest functions of the P-S process that could be categorized according to priority, method, and outcome. A latent analysis focusing especially upon dysfunctional aspects of the P-S process would probably list for priority, quantity over quality; for method, large caseloads; and for outcome, minimal interaction.

Notes

[1]Howard S. Becker, The Outsiders (New York: Free Press, 1963), p. 20.

[2]Gordon Allport and Leo Postman, The Psychology of Rumor (New York: Holt, Rinehart & Winston, 1947).

[3]See David Matza, Delinquency and Drift (New York: John Wiley, 1966) wherein Matza proposes a "middle of the road" theory combining the concepts of the classical school of criminology with concepts of the positivist school of criminology. It does seem logical that all sane persons are able to exercise choice, but may have limitations upon the degree to which they can do so. These limitations may stem from social pressures to which the individual falls victim.

[4]Jerome Skolnick, Justice Without Trial (New York: John Wiley, 1966). According to Skolnick, police officers have a degree of confidence in their judgments and interpretations that they feel justifies their predictions of behavior not yet witnessed.

[5]For a comprehensive discussion of "attribution" studies, see Baron and Byrne (1981), pp. 57-79.

[6]Ibid., pp. 118-129. These authors review the evidence showing that attitudes and behavior are responsible for a mutual cause-effect relationship. Attitudes can be seen as determinants of behavior ("we do what we believe"); and behavior is a determinant of attitudes ("we believe what we do"). See also Leon Festinger, A Theory of Cognitive Dissonance (Evanston, Ill.: Row Peterson, 1957); Leon Festinger and J. M. Carlsmith, "Cognitive Consequences of Forced Compliance," Journal of Abnormal and Social Psychology 58 (1959): 203-10.

[7]Gordon Allport, Becoming (New Haven: Yale University Press, 1955). Opportunistic learning is accomplished through conditioning, whereas propriate learning involves the internalization of values supporting the desired behavior.

[8]Baron and Byrne (1981), pp. 229-30.

[9]Solomon Asch, "Studies of Independence and Conformity I. A Minority of One Against a Unanimous Majority," Psychological Monographs 70 (1956): whole no. In a series of experiments with variations introduced, Asch was able to show how individuals will or will not admit that they perceived the length of a line differently than did the majority of their peers. Muzafer Sherif, "An Experimental Approach to the Study of Attitudes," Sociometry 1 (1937): 90-98. Here, subjects showed their agreement with one another as to the degree of movement and the direction of movement that they witnessed while exposed to the "autokinetic effect." They had been in fact viewing a stationary pinpoint of light in a dark room with no external points of reference. The optical illusion occurs causing subjects to think that they had seen the light move. In the company of another subject (or subjects), there is announced consensus (conformity) about specifics of the supposed movement.

[10]While it is recognized that the relatively new concept of the "open classroom" is a step away from these particular norms, there is agreement with Robert Dreeben, On What Is Learned in School (Reading, MA.: Addison-Wesley Publishing Co., 1968), pp. 63-86, that the atmosphere of the traditional classroom indoctrinates the individual into strict adherence to these norms. See Joan Luxenburg, "Structural Provisions for Normative Learning: Traditional and Open Classrooms," Scholar and Educator (Fall, 1978): 22-30.

[11]Albert K. Cohen, Delinquent Boys (Glencoe: Free Press, 1955).

[12]The term "situational criminal" is being used here specific to the definition formulated by Haskell and Yablonsky, pp. 273-274. This criminal type represents the individual who is confronted with a problem for which he/she seeks a solution through the commission of a crime. He/she is apprehended and given the status of criminal. However, until the time of the offense, he/she had been committed to a non-criminal value system. Because of the pressure felt upon him/her by a new situation, he/she disregards prior commitment to a normative value system.

[13]Followers of Cesare Beccaria's classical school of criminology believe that the individual, through his/her own "free will," weighs the prospective benefits of his/her actions, and compares this to the possible consequences. He/she then chooses to act or to resign himself/herself to deterrence.

[14]According to Ernest Q. Campbell, Socialization: Culture and Personality (Dubuque: Wm. C. Brown Co., 1975), p. 76, "resocialization" does require an "unlearning" process and a "relearning" process. According to Campbell's definition of resocialization, persons with antisocial attitudes have acquired skills and values which are inappropriate for the societal roles that these individuals are expected to play. Other definitions may not stress the fact that unlearning is part of the resocialization process. It is the writer's view that the inappropriate skills and values have to be unlearned, rather than simply "replaced."

[15]See Harry Wasserman, "The Professional Social Worker in a Bureaucracy," Social Work 16 (January, 1971): 99-100, for a discussion of the relative powerlessness felt by social service workers when their administrators fail to recognize client needs over organizational needs.

Chapter IV

CASE HISTORIES

On the Purposes and Limitations
of Case Histories[1]

The primary purpose for the use of case histories is to illustrate the P-S process when the process is implemented. A description of the elements constituting the P-S process model would not be complete without an anecdotal demonstration of the dynamics of the model. The case histories serve to accomplish this purpose.

In this chapter a criminal classification is developed. The specific cases which have been chosen to represent each of the categories are obviously not in a true sense "representative" of all cases which fall into each categorical type. However, the cases need not be representative for the present utilization of them. In their text, Delinquency and the Juvenile Justice System, authors Daniel Katkin, Drew Hyman, and John Kramer preface their presentation of case histories by the following remark:

> The cases discussed are not necessarily representative; indeed, the very point of this chapter is that any of these cases might have been concluded differently had they come to the attention of different policemen, or had they been heard before different judges, or had they involved different lawyers or social workers or had the children involved had different personalities or social characteristics.[2]

These authors have said much to qualify the fact that their case histories are not "representative." They then go on to recount the personal stories of eight cases, ranging from murder to absconsion from home. In doing so, these authors illustrate the diversity of procedures within the juvenile justice systems of several states. In much the same way (and with the same stipulations), this writer employs personal histories to illustrate the range of uses of the P-S process and to sustain the elements of the formulated P-S process model.

Erikson is another author who had felt able to comment that the cases presented by him in Childhood and Society are justified in their lack of representativeness:

The cases presented are not typical: in the daily run of the clinical mill, few cases demonstrate such dramatic and clear cut 'beginnings'....But we did not stray too far from clinical, and indeed historical habit when, for the purposes of demonstration, we chose cases which highlight in an unusually dramatic way the principles governing the usual.[3]

Apparently Erikson has called forth recognition for a category of case histories that could appropriately be labelled the "dramatic case history." Cases in this type of category would not be modal, typical, average, representative, etc. Rather, cases would be dramatic, using the unusual to highlight the usual. The cases used here are neither completely usual nor unusual, but lie somewhere in between. For the writer's specified use of the case history method, the cases need not be either usual or unusual.

Participant Observation Combined with Case History Presentation

Katkin, Hyman, and Kramer had borrowed five of their eight case histories from a documentary film prepared by someone other than themselves. Two other case histories, which these authors reported, came from state law case documentation. One of their cases was actually observed by the authors in a juvenile court. This writer's particular problem is that there is a need to show an objective illustration of the writer's own formulation of the P-S process model, but with case histories involving the writer as the probation officer. Undoubtedly, the first-hand involvement with the cases has had a special influence upon the writer's interaction with the offenders. This circumstance was caused by the writer's anticipation of using case histories for later documentation. Each time that the writer met a new case individual, the individual was viewed as a potential case history for the study.

The special influence felt upon the cases served for the most part to enhance the thoroughness in including as much information as possible in the case re-

66

ports. In doing so, perhaps the writer spent more time with the case and asked more in-depth questions during the presentence investigation than would other probation officers. It is possible that the over-involvement in accumulating information was seen by offenders as a devotion to helping them. If so, some may have responded with more cooperation than they would have given to an abrupt, hurried probation officer.

The fundamental question to be asked here is whether the admittedly special attention given to these clients has interfered with the purpose for which the case histories are now being used. If the content of the case histories serves only to illustrate the dynamics of the formulated P-S process model, then the closeness to the cases does not detract from their contribution to the present study.

One can recognize the "convenience" that the writer enjoyed in being able to formulate a P-S process model (after already having experienced the P-S process through the case histories)--and then being able to turn to the case histories to sustain the elements of the model. The theory and verification of theory may seem somewhat circular in logic. However, the scientific method in sociology is viewed as including both deductive and inductive logic and allowing for entrance into its process at any of its stages. The chart in Figure 2 can be used to trace the steps.[4]

The combination of participant observation and case history presentation has taken the following course. The writer had worked as a practitioner within the P-S process for six years, thus gathering some opinions from data observed. Because the research is observational, the data was not quantified, e.g., through scaling and measuring. The study was, therefore, approached with "empirical generalizations" about the way in which the P-S process is allowed to operate. The empirical generalizations were derived from on-the-job training, departmental directives, interaction with clients, interaction with other probation officers, etc. The "collection of data" was heavily weighted by the accumulation of six years' worth of case histories. From the empirical generalizations, the writer then began to theorize. Most researchers probably begin their work by theorizing; but this writer arrived at theory inductively from observations. The theorizing led to the formulation of a P-S process model which was assumed to have some resemblances to other accepted models of socialization. The writer then deduced from the proposed P-S process model a set of relationships among elements within the model. Without any "formal" hypothesis testing in this qualitative study, it was informally suggested (through a descriptive-analytic account) that any of the case histories could bear the writer out in illustrating the assumptions about the P-S process as a model. The writer needed only to concisely present one case history per offender type to sustain the elements proposed in the P-S process model. It remains possible, however, that one could challenge the writer as to whether there are any cases not presented that could contradict the model. A careful review of all of the unused cases indicates that they are all supporting the priority, outcome, and method of the model. Some cases support the model more fully than do other cases. But the degree to which a case supports the model was not used as a factor in choosing the sample. After developing a criminal classification, the writer simply chose (from all of the case histories) those cases that clearly showed the dynamics of the model. The choice of cases represents a purposive sample. Normally, such freedom in selection would skew the results of a study. However, the use of the non-representative case history has already been explained. The cases are illustrative of the model and, therefore, can be chosen.

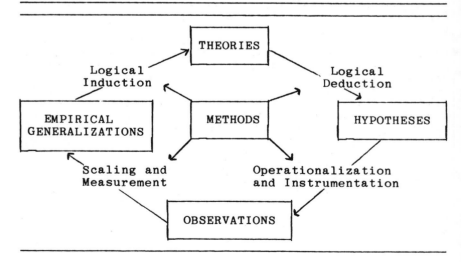

Figure 2. The scientific method in sociology.

Developing a Criminal Classification
for Selection of Case Histories

Before presenting the ten case histories, a rationale will be provided for the choice of the specific categories of offenders. In formulating the classification, certain offender types were immediately eliminated, for practical reasons. For instance, the writer never had an opportunity to work with cases involving political criminals, corporate white-collar criminals, organized crime figures, and "professional criminals."[5] The writer had been confined to working with misdemeanants. However, not every type of charge represented in the misdemeanor section of Metropolitan Area's penal code will be listed here. Some probationers, whose cases are presented, had involved themselves in a variety of offenses over a period of time. Because one case history is categorized as an "auto thief (repeater)," does not mean that one cannot take into account the subject's past arrest for store burglary. If one were to cross-reference past offenses within the case histories, one would arrive at a figure greater than ten criminal types.

Three sources from the literature have been combined for devising the criminal classification. The first source is Haskell and Yablonsky's categories of laws based upon the degree of public consensus for apprehension, prosecution, and strict reprisals for persons breaking laws.[6] These authors categorize laws in the following manner:

1. laws restating mores;
2. laws reinforcing mores and folkways;
3. laws formalizing folkways.

Category (1) offenses include murder, forcible rape, robbery, larceny, burglary, assault, etc. Prohibitions against these behaviors have been with us since the Ten Commandments. Thus, this category is also referred to as "traditional crime." An offense in this category is considered "mala in se" (bad in itself). The public holds the strongest consensus of opinion in calling for apprehension, prosecution, and penalties for offenders in this category. In addition to the clamor for the application of formal, negative sanctions, the public applies its own informal, negative sanctions toward offenders in this category. In contrast, category (2) offenses are not bad in themselves, but are "mala prohibita" (bad because they have been prohibited). Offenses in this category include indecent exposure, obscene exhibitionism, prostitution, drug abuse, gambling, etc. A majority of offenses in this category are "victimless crimes."[7] The public privately engages in much of this behavior on a widescale basis. The definitions of deviant and immoral behavior are obscure due to many "norms of evasion." The public, therefore, is segmented in its degree of support for apprehension, prosecution, and penalties for offenders in this category. Even those who choose not to engage in certain of these behaviors find that they can tolerate others engaging in the behavior. The public, therefore, does not necessarily apply informal, negative sanctions to perpetrators in this category. Category (3) offenses are breaches of agreed upon codes of conduct, specific to certain situations or occupations. Examples of offenses in this category include infractions of some sections of motor vehicle codes, labor codes, health and safety codes, and business and professional codes. Unless the public feels directly involved with the offender, the public tends to be less concerned about the apprehension, prosecution, and penalties for offenders in this category. In the case of motor vehicle codes, the public sometimes identifies and empathizes with the unfortunate rule-breaker who gets caught. Often, a motorist reduces his/her own excessive speed as he/she witnesses someone else stopped by police for speeding. The thought taking place in the passing motorist's mind is "there but for the grace of luck go I." The writer does not mean to imply that no one wants motor vehicle codes enforced. Of course, people feel safe in knowing that while they are on the road, others are following the rules of the road. It is rare, however, for the public to apply any informal, negative sanctions toward offenders in this category. All three of Haskell and Yablonsky's categories differ with regard to the degree of enmity perceived by the public between itself and the law violator.

Before mentioning the other two sources from which the criminal classification is derived, it is appropriate to name the categories of offenders represented by the ten case histories, and show the relationship of the categories to Haskell and Yablonsky's schema. The following are the labels affixed to the case histories:

1. Sociopathic Offender;
2. Robber;
3. Assaultist (Repeater);

4. Auto Thief (Repeater);
5. White-Collar Criminal (Employee Theft);
6. Drug Addict 1;
7. Drug Addict 2;[8]
8. Nonviolent Sex Offender;
9. Statutory Rapist;
10. Intoxicated Driver (Repeater).

The first five offenders have broken laws restating mores. It should be noted that the sociopathic offender had been on probation for the charge of petit larceny, which in itself puts him into Haskell and Yablonsky's first category. Discussion of his case focuses upon his past behavior (which recurred while he was on probation)--forcible rape. This charge would also justify the sociopathic offender's inclusion into the category of laws restating mores. In addition to the first five offenders, one of the drug addicts had been placed on probation for circumstances surrounding a stolen check. She, therefore, could be placed into the category of laws restating mores. However, her addiction problem is focused upon, thereby placing her into Haskell and Yablonsky's second category--laws reinforcing mores and folkways. The sixth and seventh case histories (both drug addicts), the eighth case (indecent exposure or "public lewdness") and the ninth case (statutory rape) all fall under the category of laws reinforcing mores and folkways. The tenth case history (intoxicated driver) falls into Haskell and Yablonsky's third category--laws formalizing folkways. The chart in Table 10 illustrates where these offender types are placed according to Haskell and Yablonsky's categories of laws and public consensus as to the degree of severity for the application of formal and informal, negative sanctions.

TABLE 10

CRIMINAL CLASSIFICATION I

Laws Restating Mores	Laws Reinforcing Mores and Folkways	Laws Formalizing Folkways
Sociopathy (forcible rape) Robbery Assault Larceny (auto) (white-collar crime, employee theft)	Drug Addiction Public Lewdness Statutory Rape	Intoxicated Driving

The second source turned to in developing the criminal classification, is the taxonomy provided by Marshall B. Clinard and Richard Quinney.[9] Haskell and Yablonsky's categories are less complex than Clinard and Quinney's. Haskell and Yablonsky's division of laws is based on the criterion of public reaction. Clinard and Quinney present the following five theoretical dimensions for a typology of criminal behavior:

1. Legal Aspects of Selected Offenses;
2. Criminal Career of the Offender;
3. Group Support of Criminal Behavior;
4. Correspondence Between Criminal and Legitimate Behavior;
5. Societal Reaction and Legal Processing.

From these five considerations, Clinard and Quinney construct nine types of criminal behavior:
1. Violent Personal Criminal Behavior;
2. Occasional Property Criminal Behavior;
3. Public Order Criminal Behavior;
4. Conventional Criminal Behavior;
5. Political Criminal Behavior;
6. Occupational Criminal Behavior;
7. Corporate Criminal Behavior;
8. Organized Criminal Behavior;
9. Professional Criminal Behavior.

Of Clinard and Quinney's nine categories of offender types, categories (5), (7), (8), and (9) have already been eliminated by the writer as prospects for case histories, because the writer had no opportunity to deal with offenders occupying these statuses. These types of offenders are encountered by Metropolitan Area's Supreme Court (criminal) division. As previously mentioned, the writer's Criminal Court division dealt with only misdemeanor cases.

What Haskell and Yablonsky refer to as laws restating mores correspond to Clinard and Quinney's categories (1), (2), (4), and (6) offenders. Category (1) offenses (violent personal criminal behavior), according to Clinard and Quinney, include homicide, assault, and forcible rape. Category (2) offenses (occasional property criminal behavior) include forgery, shoplifting, vandalism, and auto theft (but not on a "professional criminal" basis). Category (4) offenses (conventional criminal behavior), like category (2) offenses, involve violation of property, but are oriented toward the goal of economic success and tend to be career crimes. These include larceny, burglary, and robbery. Category (6) offenses (occupational criminal behavior) is described by Clinard and Quinney, but with no specific examples provided. It would appear that these offenses are infractions of rules governing the practices of certain occupational groups. It appears that the groups tend to be of legitimate, professional, and high status. Probably embezzlement by an executive would fit the description better than would the small-scale salesclerk embezzler. Nonetheless, because no specific examples of offenders in this category are mentioned by Clinard and Quinney, the case history of a salesclerk embezzler will be included, because the crime was committed during the course of her occupational duties. The writer has chosen not to include the above-mentioned case history under the category of conventional larceny. According to Clinard and Quinney, conventional larceny is career-oriented and centers around economic success. Category (2) offenses (occasional property offender) may actually be the most appropriate for the salesclerk embezzler, because the offense of shoplifting is included in this category. The young lady represented in the case history had been committing pilferage of goods from the store in which she had been employed. Further, the pilferer thought that she was justified in engaging in this behavior because it was her understanding that all of her co-workers were doing the same. Clinard and Quinney remark that occasional property offenders "do not usually conceive of themselves as criminals and are able to rationalize their criminal behavior."[10]

73

What Haskell and Yablonsky refer to as laws reinforcing mores and folkways may be found to coincide
with what Clinard and Quinney refer to as category (3)
offenses (public order criminal behavior). These offenses include prostitution, homosexuality, drunkenness, and drug use.

The writer has not found a category of Clinard
and Quinney's that would coincide with Haskell and
Yablonsky's laws formalizing folkways. It is true that
this category of Haskell and Yablonsky's does include
professional and business codes. Therefore, that one
aspect can be related to Clinard and Quinney's category
(6) offenses (occupational criminal behavior). However, it is unclear as to where Clinard and Quinney
would place offenses that constitute infractions of the
motor vehicle code. They do place "drunkenness" in
category (3) offenses (public order criminal behavior).
Therefore, perhaps intoxicated driving is a "public order" offense. A case history of an intoxicated driver
will be presented. Haskell and Yablonsky have provided
the rationale to include this criminal type. Therefore, Haskell and Yablonsky's schema has been helpful
in extending Clinard and Quinney's categories.

The chart in Table 11 illustrates where Clinard
and Quinney's categories are placed with respect to
Haskell and Yablonsky's categories. The offender types
that constitute the writer's case histories are represented in parentheses.

The third and last source which has been tapped
to organize the classification is provided by Don C.
Gibbons.[11] Gibbons presents a typology of fifteen
patterns of adult criminal behavior.

1. Professional Thief;
2. Professional "Heavy" Criminal;
3. Semi-Professional Property Criminal;
4. Property Offender--"One-Time Loser";
5. Automobile Thief--"Joyrider";
6. Naive Check Forger;
7. White-Collar Criminal;
8. Professional "Fringe" Violator;
9. Embezzler;
10. Personal Offender--"One-Time Loser";
11. "Psychopathic" Assaultist;
12. Violent Sex Offender;
13. Nonviolent Sex Offender;
14. Nonviolent Sex Offender--Statutory Rape;
15. Narcotic Addict--Heroin.

TABLE 11

CRIMINAL CLASSIFICATION II

Laws Restating Mores	Laws Reinforcing Mores and Folkways	Laws Formalizing Folkways
Violent Personal Offender (sociopathy-- forcible rape) (assault)	Public Order Criminal (drug addiction) (public lewdness) (statutory rape)	Public Order Criminal (intoxicated driving)
Occasional Property Criminal (auto theft) (white-collar crime--employee theft)		
Conventional Criminal (robbery)		
Occupational Criminal (white-collar crime--employee theft)		

Categories (1), (2), and (8) are immediately eliminated from the discussion, as these are cases that the writer never encountered. Gibbons himself points out that types (1) and (2) (professionals) "are infrequently encountered in treatment caseloads because of considerable crime skill exhibited by incumbents of these categories."[12] As for category (8) offenders (professional "fringe" violator), Gibbons defines this type through what Gibbons believes to be its best example--the illegal abortionist.[13] The writer had no opportunity to work with this type of offender.

With regard to the twelve relevant categories that are left, the divisions between some merely refer to the regularity with which the same type of crime is committed. For instance, if one combines categories (4) and (5) offenders (property offender--"one-time loser"--and automobile thief--"joyrider"), one is able to refer to the case history of an automobile thief (repeater). Other categorical divisions can be overcome by cross-references of different offenses within a single case history. Category (3) can be combined with category (10) to refer to the case history of a robber. According to Gibbons, category (3) offenders (semi-professional property criminals):

> engage in strong-arm robberies, holdups, burglaries, larcenies, and other similar direct assaults upon personal or private property. . . .Strong-arm robbery does not involve much detailed planning and careful execution of the crime, but rather the application of crude physical force in order to relieve a victim of his money.[14]

According to Gibbons, category (10) offenses (personal offender--"one-time loser") includes murder, negligent manslaughter, and serious assaults. However, normally the offense takes place against a victim who is related to, or well known to, the offender.[15] Therefore, although the label personal offender--"one-time loser"-- may sound appropriate for the case history of a robber, category (3), of the semi-professional property offender, best stands alone to describe this particular case history.

Category (6)--naive check forger--and cate (12)--violent sex offender--are behaviors which, when combined, describe the case history of a sociopathic offender. Although category (11) is labelled "psychopathic assaultist," it neither fits the case history of a sociopath nor the case history of an assaultist repeater. After having read Gibbons' description of a psychopathic assaultist, the need to include a habitual assaultist as a case history became apparent. However, not all assault repeaters are psychopathic. Specifically, Gibbons refers to the psychopathic assaultist as one who, when committing property offenses, becomes involved in such offenses "frequently accompanied by violent acts in which his coercive and violent actions are essentially senseless."[16] According to Gibbons, the psychopathic assaultist is "feared by other inmates because of that offender's asocial and violent disposition."[17]

The assaultist repeater represented in the case history is not psychopathic, but is merely someone trying to prove his manliness through physical altercations, under conditions that he feels provoked him. The case history of a sociopathic offender does refer to "sexual assaults"; however, these were not of a violent nature. They are labelled assaultive, because they were committed under threat. The writer's use of the term "sociopath" will be clarified here. The label "sociopath" is now accepted by the American Psychiatric Association, used interchangeably with the term "psychopath." The case example had not been officially diagnosed as a sociopath; however, he holds many of the diagnostic characteristics. For more information about the characteristics of a sociopathic personality, criminal behavior of the sociopath, etiology of sociopathy, and treatment of sociopathy, William and Arline McCord present a comprehensive discussion.[18] Personality characteristics include chronically asocial, driven by uncontrolled desires, highly impulsive, aggressive, feels little or no guilt, unable to profit from experience or punishment, callous, extremely hedonistic, unable to form lasting bonds of affection with other human beings, unable to maintain loyalties to persons or codes, moral imbecility, insincere, untrustworthy, improvident, no capacity for automatic self-punishment, defective conscience, unable to appreciate the reactions of others to his/her behavior, lacks remorse (although he/she may express it), lacks capacity for the "looking-glass self," unexplained failure (e.g., undisturbed technical intelligence), absence of neurotic anxiety, persistent and inadequately motivated antisocial behavior, irresponsibility, peculiar inability to distinguish between truth and falsehood, inability to accept blame, inappropriate or fantastic reactions to alcohol, lacks insight, shallow and impersonal responses to sexual life, often threatens suicide (but rarely carries it out), persistent pattern of self-defeat, etc. Criminal behavior is characterized as short-sighted in that the crimes are for kicks or are for low stakes at high risks. Common crimes committed by sociopaths include petty fraud, theft, rape, etc. The cause of sociopathy may be a social one, such as child abuse, child neglect, faulty socialization, etc. The cause may be a neurological impairment due to encephalitis, brain injury, hypothalamic malfunctioning, etc. Treatment is usually unsuccessful. Sociopaths do not respond to legal punishment, even though they do learn opportunistically to try to avoid punishment. Psychodrama may be the best treatment for sociopaths under age fifteen. As a group therapy, psychodrama provides an atmosphere for development of the "looking-glass self" through the use of role reversal. It also provides a catharsis for safely, dramatically letting out hostility. These characteristics clearly expand Gibbons' concept of the psychopathic offender.

Gibbons' categories (7) and (9)--white-collar criminal and embezzler--refer to the case history of a white-collar criminal (employee theft). Gibbons defines embezzlement as "stealing from the employer"; and yet, he states that embezzlement is "not properly classified as white-collar crime."[19] However, the originator of the concept of white-collar crime, Edwin H. Sutherland, had specified that "breaches of trust" during the course of one's occupation constitute white-collar crime.[20]

Category (8) of nonviolent sex offender will be presented in a case history which bears the same categorical label. According to Gibbons, this category includes exhibitionism, child molesting, and incest. Noteworthy is the interactional setting which Gibbons associates with the offense of exhibitionism. According to Gibbons:

> victims are usually persons unknown to the offender, chosen somewhat randomly. Exhibitionism tends to occur at places where female observers are likely to be present-- at schools, parks, and the like.[21]

A case history of an exhibitionist who fits this pattern will be provided.

Category (15) of nonviolent sex offender--statutory rape--refers to the case history of a statutory rapist. This type of offense, which already has been referred to as falling within Haskell and Yablonsky's laws reinforcing mores and folkways, is characterized by Gibbons similarly. According to Gibbons, statutory rapists do not perceive of themselves as criminals, but:

> view themselves as unlucky persons who were simply doing what everyone else is doing, but who got caught. There is of course considerable truth in that claim. . . .They are essentially law-abiding citizens who have fallen into the hands of the police and courts for technically illegal but culturally widespread acts.[22]

The case history of a statutory rapist depicts the above definition.

Category (15) of narcotic addict--heroin--refers to one of the drug addict case histories. The other drug addict case history concerns an addiction to methadone. Two separate case histories for the one category of drug addiction were chosen for presentation because of the diversity displayed by offenders in this category. Gibbons notes that drug addiction is usually accompanied by other forms of crime, in order to gain money to buy the drug. One of the case histories had come to the court's attention because of a stolen, forged check. The other drug addict case history represents someone who was apprehended when he was acting out his "high." It should also be noted that the case history of a robber represents someone who had committed robbery in order to support his heroin habit. Gibbons further notes that some addicts view their use of drugs as "a relatively innocuous, personal vice which should not be regarded as criminal in nature."[23] This latter comment strengthens the position of Haskell and Yablonsky for having classified drug use as a violation of laws reinforcing mores and folkways.

Having exhausted Gibbons' typology of criminals, the writer is able to account for only eight of the case histories. The habitual assaultist cannot actually fit into Gibbons' schema (for reasons previously stated here). As far as the case history of an intoxicated driver is concerned, the writer cannot find any of Gibbons' fifteen categories that would encompass an

offender of this type. However, the two previous
sources of typologies justify inclusion of this particular criminal category.

After having examined the three sources of criminal typologies, the writer chose to not continue the
search through the other typologies presented in the
literature.[24] It should be noted that most criminal
typologies are created to explain and typify categories
of behavior. The needs of the present study are served
by merely having an array of types of criminal behavior
to illustrate how the different criminal types can in-
teract with the P-S process. Combining the three
sources, the nine criminal types are derived (with two
separate kinds of drug addiction), thus establishing a
classification for ten case history presentations.

The remainder of this chapter provides the reader
with an anecdotal demonstration of the P-S process.
The ten case histories are presented, each followed by
a brief analysis of the P-S process implemented. The
brevity of case analysis allows the reader to engage in
his/her own exercise in analysis. The reader may want
to partake in a dissection of each case and apply casework techniques for further discussion than has been
attempted here. (As stated in the preface, names and
other identifying labels in the cases have been changed
in order to preserve the anonymity of the subjects.)

Case History of a Sociopathic Offender

In November of 1974, Harold G. (age twenty-nine)
was placed on probation for a three-year period for the
charge petit larceny (a last of a series of offenses
dating from his juvenile years). Specifically, Harold
admittedly had taken a check from his employer's office
(Handy Packaging Corp.) and made the check payable to
himself for $166.83. Harold collected said amount by
cashing the check. The employer pressed charges after
discovering the cancelled check returned to him. At
the time that the charges had been filed, Harold was in
the employ of another firm, having left Handy Packaging
Corp. of his own accord.

During the probation department's investigation,
Harold appeared cooperative and remorseful. He explained the factors leading up to the offense. Harold
stated that he had been in financial need. He had promised his wife a trip to a nearby state and he did not
want to disappoint her. He felt pressured into obtain-

ing money quickly. Harold committed the offense without his wife's knowledge. Harold had the key to his employer's office and used it for the offense while the employer was on vacation. Harold did consider the likelihood of being detected; but, he decided to leave the matter to luck or fate. The amount of the check did not coincide with any figure that Harold would be entitled to as an employee. The firm was small enough to allow the employer to recognize the check when it was returned to him as cancelled. Although Harold had left the firm one week after the offense, his mother-in-law remained employed there.

Harold reported the following personal history to the probation department: Harold had been adopted as an out-of-wedlock child and raised by Mr. and Mrs. G. who have been deceased three years and two years, respectively. Mr. G. had been a railroad conductor. Harold's adoptive parents had known Harold's natural mother prior to Harold's birth and had taken Harold into their care immediately after his birth. Harold did not hear about his adoption until he was age twenty-one; however, he did suspect it prior to being informed by his adoptive parents. Harold met his natural mother, but was reluctant to discuss her with the probation department. The adoptive parents had two natural children who were adults and out of the home while Harold was being reared. Harold had no contact with these siblings who were in their forties and fifties. Harold married Sally R. less than a year before his contact with the probation department. Harold and Sally had known each other for one-and-a-half years prior to their marriage. They resided in an apartment next door to Sally's parents.

Sally was interviewed by the probation department. Sally (age twenty-five) was employed as a freight forwarder; however, she holds a B.A. in English and had hopes of entering law school in the future. Sally appeared to be very supportive of Harold. Harold, who had an eighth-grade education, appeared to be less mature in his thinking and less intelligent than Sally. While Harold's physical appearance was average, Sally appeared to be less physically appealing.

Harold had been employed as a lab technician in an eyeglass firm for four months at the time of his sentencing for the offense. He was earning $100 per week net. Previous employment had been sporadic.

Harold had a previous history with the courts. Harold reported a history of several contacts with the juvenile court. He advised the probation officer that these court involvements concerned thefts. Harold further informed the probation officer that he had been sent as a juvenile to Pleasantland State Hospital (a mental institution). Harold was too uneasy about discussing the nature of this commitment. He signed a consent form for us to obtain this report. We requested a report, but received no reply. Regarding Harold's previous adult arrests, we had a record of four. Harold gave his version of each of these offenses. On April 2, 1962, Harold had been arrested regarding a stolen auto. He was granted "youthful offender" status and confined for three years. On December 21, 1967, Harold was arrested concerning another stolen auto. He received "time served" on a plea of guilty on March 3, 1969, after having been at Heavenly State Hospital for the Criminally Insane from May 8, 1968 to January 16, 1969. Harold was also too uneasy with the probation officer to discuss this commitment. He signed a consent form for us to obtain the record. We did receive a one-page summary several months after Harold had been placed on probation. The hospital summary also referred to a subsequent admission. The report was descriptive of uneventful hospital stays. There was no mention of specific reasons for the admissions. There was no diagnosis mentioned. On May 18, 1969, Harold was arrested for sodomy. On March 20, 1972, this case was dismissed after Harold had been at Heavenly State Hospital and transferred later to Downtown State Hospital, a cumulative hospital stay of approximately three years. (The hospital summary, previously referred to, covered this admission and discharge, but without referring to any specific presenting problem.) Harold told the probation officer little about this arrest other than the fact that it concerned a nine-year old girl who had lived within the same apartment building as Harold. The only remark that Harold was able to make regarding this case was "they couldn't prove it." On March 11, 1973, Harold was arrested for attempted rape, sodomy, possession of a dangerous weapon, and menacing. On March 29, 1973, Harold received a conditional discharge for this case. According to Harold, this case resulted from his having had intercourse and other sexual acts with a fifteen-year old girl in his apartment. Harold claimed that the girl gave her consent and had told Harold that she was nineteen years old. Harold claimed that the girl filed the complaint in retaliation after she found that she could not get any drugs from Harold (who had no drug involvement). Regarding the dangerous weapon charge, Harold claimed that he had a knife in the room, on his dresser, that was visible to the girl; but Harold denied having threatened the girl with it.

It should be noted that Sally knew nothing about Harold's arrest history, other than the fact that he had been sent away as a youth regarding a stolen auto. Sally did know that Harold had been in a mental institution. In fact it was Sally who told the probation officer that she knew through Harold's maternal aunt that Harold had attempted suicide while at Heavenly State Hospital. Sally did know about another court involvement in which Harold had been the complainant. In view of Harold's history of sexual assault, this case was of interest to us and was of a suspicious nature. According to Harold, in June of 1973 he was stabbed in the chest nine times by a female prostitute in a downtown area park. He required hospitalization for pierced heart arteries, etc. The woman was arrested at the scene. As a result of the attack, Harold pressed charges against the female in County A Supreme Court. Harold was unable to tell the probation officer the woman's name, nor any documenting details that would help the probation officer to check the court records. Harold claimed that he did not pursue the case because he moved from County A to County B. (These two locations are just a few minutes apart from each other; and there are no mitigating circumstances that come into being when a complainant moves from one county to another within Metropolitan Area.) Further, Harold did not keep follow-up appointments at the hospital after his discharge, although he did suffer occasional chest pains and breathing complications requiring attention elsewhere. As to why the attack had taken place, Harold claimed that he had refused the woman's propositions and she retaliated with a knife.

With all of the above history known to the court, Harold was placed on probation (as per our recommendation) for three years on two special conditions: (1) to pay $166.80 restitution, and (2) to become involved in psychiatric therapy if directed by the probation department.

After a few contacts with Harold, we formulated a plan for treatment (under probation supervision) that revolved around employment, finances, and a careful accounting of leisure time activities.

83

Harold was periodically unemployed. He left his job at the optical firm due to a fight between him and another male employee. Harold had known the other worker on a social basis also, e.g., having double-dated occasionally. Harold reported a previous physical altercation with the same co-worker at Harold's apartment building. At that time, Harold admitted that he had pulled a knife on the other fellow. The probation officer directed Harold not to carry the knife which he claimed to have needed for cleaning callouses on his hands. Harold agreed to dispose of the knife. It was typical of Harold to report any new circumstance to the probation officer, as well as to display a cooperative attitude. Sally usually accompanied Harold to our office for an unscheduled visit to report a problem, e.g., such as the loss of a job, etc. It might be said that compared to other probationers, Harold was overly cautious about his contacts with the probation department. Regarding the special conditions of probation, Harold paid the restitution within his two-month deadline, although he and Sally were barely able to "make ends meet." As for the psychiatric therapy, initially we did not direct Harold for therapy, because the brief Heavenly-Downtown State Hospitals' summary made no recommendation for same. (Much later in our contact, when conditions warranted it, we directed Harold to begin therapy.)

It was difficult to justify to Sally why the probation officer was continuously asking about Harold's evenings. It was learned that the couple agreed that Harold could have an evening to himself every week. The probation officer found this to be unusual, since Harold had no planned activity to take part in. Several months after Harold had been placed on probation, a rather suspicious incident was reported by Harold. He appeared for a scheduled visit in our office with lacerations over most of his face. Harold provided the following explanation for his appearance: He was driving through the "east end of town" (a seedy part of Hippie Haven) and was attacked by an unknown black male. This is said to have occurred when Harold stopped for a red light. The assailant allegedly reached into Harold's opened car window brandishing a knife, with which he wounded Harold's face in several places. The probation officer asked Harold if he had reported the incident to the local police precinct which was located three blocks away from the scene of the incident. Harold acknowledged the exact location of the precinct; but he had chosen not to report the crime. He stated that he did not know the reason for the attack and did not feel that the police could be of help. The probation officer asked Harold if he had received treatment for the wounds at the nearby City Hospital. Harold chose instead to drive back to County B to receive stitches at another City Hospital emergency room. He had chosen this thirty-minute drive for no explainable reason. He also had reported to the emergency room that the wounds were caused by a sudden stop in his car causing his face to go through the windshield. Clearly, the incident was suspicious because it seems to be a purposeful avoidance of police and hospital services in the neighborhood in which the incident occurred.

The next incident of concern was a re-arrest for an attempted rape allegation. Harold and Sally appeared for an unscheduled visit as soon as our office opened one morning. They explained that an incident had occurred on the previous evening which was likely to result in a re-arrest. Harold was being accused (by an eighteen-year old female) of attempted rape and assault with a knife. Harold's version was the following: Harold had befriended a sixteen-year old neighborhood boy. Through the boy, Harold met the boy's eighteen-year old sister. Sally also got to know them both. (As an aside, we had records for both the brother and sister in our office as they had been known to our office as Persons In Need of Supervision. Their cases had been terminated. However, the probation officer consulted the files to learn that both had been school truants but exhibited no antisocial behavior. Further, the girl had been described as quite attractive.) For several days prior to the alleged incident, Harold had been giving the girl a ride to her evening job, as her car was being repaired. Her brother came along for the ride. On the only day that the brother failed to accompany Harold and the girl, the incident is said to have occurred. The girl called Sally's mother and reported the following: Harold had driven her to a local "parking spot," a meeting place for lovers, and had made sexual advances toward her at knife point. She resisted and struggled her way nearly out of the car, whereupon Harold shoved her out of the car and sped off. In the process, she received a knife wound on her thumb, requiring stitches. Others at the scene assisted her. She reported the incident to the police and gave them Harold's name and address. In our office, Sally wanted to double check on whether a formal complaint was going to take place. Sally called the girl, from our office, and also asked the girl if she would care to repeat the story to Harold's probation officer. The girl repeated the above story to the probation officer. Harold's version differed. According to Harold, the girl was high on marihuana and was interested in making a detour on the way to work. Then she became erratic in the car. Harold had been cleaning the callouses on his hands with the same knife that the probation officer had earlier directed him to discard. Harold claimed that the girl accidentally hurt her thumb on his knife. Harold drove away from the scene after the girl ran out of his car. He then drove the car from County B to County A where he parked it in a parking lot. He did not want police to find the car near his home.

Harold and Sally were seeking advice from the probation officer, as they had not yet heard from the police. Sally was motivated to help Harold and expressed a feeling that he needed psychiatric care. Harold was motivated to avoid arrest and felt that a psychiatric hospitalization would delay, or even prevent, his otherwise imminent arrest. Each spoke to the probation officer in private as well as jointly about this. Sally informed the probation officer that Harold's natural mother had recently died and it appeared that Harold was quite depressed about it. Sally noted a kind of crudeness or roughness in Harold's sexual relations with her that she had not noticed before. Sally, having had some "pre-med" study, raised the issue that Harold may be the product of an incestuous relationship. Sally felt that this factor could be a cause of a chromosomal abnormality which in turn could be contributing to abnormal behavior. According to Sally, there was a rumor in Harold's family (mostly espoused by Harold's maternal aunt) that Harold's natural mother conceived Harold after a history of sexual intercourse with her brother. The brother was a family outcast living in another state. Sally had high hopes that the mental hygiene system would do elaborate tests of Harold based on his history and give him attention. The probation officer knew differently; however, it was felt that Harold should be evaluated by a psychiatrist. The probation officer suggested to Harold that he go directly from our office to the City Hospital and ask to have himself admitted for psychiatric observation which could eventuate in a transfer to a state hospital for care. Harold was very agreeable because he wanted to avoid an arrest. The probation officer advised Harold to provide the hospital with all of his history and to ask the hospital to contact the probation officer for supplementary information. Harold remained in the hospital for several weeks. He phoned the probation officer periodically. He would not follow the probation officer's advice to supply the examining doctor with a full history. He would not even tell the doctor about the pending allegation. He had feigned hearing voices to get admitted to the hospital. He did report depression over his natural mother's death, but he gave very little other information to the hospital. Sally had tried to see the doctor as a collateral interview and had given the probation officer's card to the doctor. She was quite frustrated that the doctor did not want to interview her nor did he contact the probation officer. The probation officer left messages for the doctor, but there were no return calls. (It should be noted that we have perceived this type of inefficiency to be typical of the area's city and state hospitals.) In the interim, a detective was in contact with Sally and with the probation officer to verify Harold's status at the hospital. The detective was reluctant to take the girl's complaint as an attempted rape; however, he had to file an assault charge in view of the stab wound. The nature of the charge allowed for Harold to receive a "desk appearance ticket" upon his release from the hospital. Harold, therefore, asked to be discharged from the hospital. He reported to the detective and appeared in court. The case was adjourned several times. During the interim, we received the discharge summary from the hospital. Since it recommended medication and psychiatric therapy through the hospital's outpatient clinic, we enforced that special condition of probation. We threatened to file a violation of probation if Harold would not attend therapy. He procrastinated, complaining of side affects of the medication. He eventually obeyed and reluctantly began therapy or at least reported to have arranged for his first appointment. At approximately the same time he was prepared to tell the court that the girl had cut her thumb on the broken fly window of his auto. Harold advised the probation officer that he had pictures of the window to show the court. He was to deny possessing the knife, on the advice of his legal aid attorney. However, at the next court appearance the girl failed to appear (for the first time); and the case was dismissed for failure to prosecute (in the absence of a complainant).

The above disposition occurred within a couple of weeks before this probation officer resigned. Therefore, this probation officer's last contact with Harold was for the purpose of reminding him that, although he could not be cited for a violation of probation for the above incident (as no conviction had occurred), he could be cited if he failed to attend therapy. The case was transferred to another probation officer for the remainder of Harold's supervision period. This probation officer had supervised him for nearly one year and had no further information about his case after the last contact with him in September of 1975. (It should be noted that the record contained a recommendation that the case not be considered for early termination under the city's new budget crisis guidelines.)

Case Analysis of a Sociopathic Offender

Harold is a classic example of someone capable of opportunistic learning. However, his ability to pursue propriate learning is doubtful. He shows the opportunistic learning by keeping appointments with his probation officer, reporting new circumstances to his probation officer, and by showing a cooperative attitude to the probation officer. His superficial awareness of societal values is demonstrated by his apparent relapse into the same behavior (rape) for which he had been treated. Since external mechanisms of socialization guide the probation officer, these are implemented by the threat of violation of probation contingent upon an infraction of the rules of probation. Harold avoided a violation of probation only because his re-arrest did not result in a conviction. His next obstacle is the direction from the probation officer to attend therapy. It is presumed that Harold will attend therapy only to avoid a violation of probation. Because he has not fully cooperated in the past with the mental hygiene system, it is expected that he will just "go through the motions" of therapy. When he had admitted himself to the City Hospital for psychiatric observation, he did so only to delay his re-arrest. He did not share any information with the hospital that would have brought him help. It is also probable that Harold recognizes that the hospital is organized in an inefficient manner that allows people like himself to dupe the system.

In Harold's case, there exists the possibility that the potential loss of his wife, Sally, might be a behavior modification contingency. The probation officer sensed that after Harold's re-arrest, Sally was questioning her marriage to Harold. A threat on her part to leave Harold possibly could have motivated Harold to seek psychiatric help. The P-S process, of course, could not instigate this particular contingency. We were not even allowed to inform Sally of previous arrests, because of professional confidentiality. It is also possible that Sally would not have been able to use herself as a reinforcer, because she may not have had a premium placed upon her by Harold. Aspects that define a sociopathic personality have already been referred to earlier. One of these aspects dealt with the inability to form affection bonds with another person. Because the sociopath is an asocial individual, the threat of the loss of a seemingly personal relationship would probably have little relevance to Harold.

External mechanisms employing the threat of loss of freedom (violation of probation) can insure a type of behavioral obedience on the part of the sociopath. However, the obedience pertains to cooperation with the regulatory procedures of the probation department only. Part of these regulatory procedures asks that the probationer not violate another law. It is not an easy task for the probation officer to prove that a probationer has broken another law. The probationer could escape the detection of police. This may have been the case when Harold suffered face lacerations while on probation. If the probationer does become apprehended, he could escape a court conviction. This was the case when Harold's re-arrest resulted in a court dismissal (because the complainant failed to appear). Therefore, the only behavioral obedience that can be maintained by the probation officer in a case such as Harold's rests on either the behavior that the probation officer can directly observe (e.g., office appointments, therapy verification, etc.); or it rests on alleged behavior that is sustained later by a court decision.

It might further be concluded that the sociopath, in general, represents a personality type that is most difficult to work with in the P-S process. His/her inability to apply an internal mechanism of control (lack of propriate learning, lack of conscience, lack of the looking-glass self, etc.) mitigates against any other efforts. The fact that the P-S process relies heavily on the external mechanism of control does not mean that the process discards completely the internal mechanisms of socialization. The P-S process gives little priority to values, when compared to behavior, out of necessity. However, since the P-S process is characterized

as a reformative effort, values are a hoped for change,
while behavior is an expected and measurable change.
Harold presents little hope for attitude change. His
behavioral change is minimal and is not affecting the
most important behavior--antisocial behavior, particularly rape.

Case History of a Robber

In April of 1970, Alfred B. (age twenty-one) was
placed on probation for a three-year period for the
charge of possession of a hypodermic instrument. A
special condition of probation was that Alfred remain
in a drug treatment program. Specifically, the arrest
was for robbery, possession of a dangerous drug, and
possession of a hypodermic needle. Alfred's version of
the offense was the following: Alfred claimed that he
walked into a liquor store simply for the purpose of
making a purchase. The store's owner questioned
Alfred's age, whereupon Alfred showed his work identification card. The card was three years old, and the
picture differed from Alfred's appearance. An argument
ensued during which Alfred struck the store owner in
the head with a wrench that Alfred had in his possession. After he struck the man, he decided to rob the
cash register, but was stopped by a passing patrolman.
Alfred admitted that a hypodermic needle and heroin
residue were found on him, as he had a heroin addiction. The probation officer reviewed the arresting
officer's written statement with Alfred. According to
the arresting officer, he was passing by the liquor
store when he saw Alfred stooping over the store owner.
The store owner, who was lying on the floor, told the
officer that Alfred had tried to rob him by hitting him
with the wrench that had been concealed in an umbrella.
The officer's statement indicated that the store owner
had died of a heart attack six days after the incident;
and the robbery complaint was, therefore, dismissed
(because of no complainant). The probation officer
asked Alfred whether he felt responsible for the man's
death; and he sadly replied that he did. Alfred maintained his version--that he had not gone into the store
for the purpose of committing robbery. He denied "con-
cealing" the wrench in the umbrella; and claimed that
he had been on his way to a friend's house to return
the wrench. Alfred advised the probation officer that
the umbrella was his and that he had carried it on that
day because of bad weather. (When the probation officer later spoke to Alfred's mother, with whom he had
been living, she told the probation officer that she

had never seen the umbrella before, and did not think that it was Alfred's.)

During the probation presentence investigation, we gathered the following personal history about Alfred (through several interviews with him and his mother, as well as through a visit to his home): Alfred was the product of a broken home wherein he was one of three children. He had a married sister (age thirty-three) and another sister (age thirty). The father had left the home when Alfred was three years old, but had been visiting Alfred until Alfred was of high school age. The father then helped finance Alfred's Catholic high school education. The mother explained that, although Alfred probably did not know the reason for the separation, the reason was that the father had been involved in homosexual relations. The mother informed the probation officer that Alfred's thirty-year old sister, who was close to the father, was hospitalized on three different occasions at three different mental institutions because of emotional problems related to sexual relationships. The mother related a sexual experience that had taken place between that daughter and Alfred when Alfred had been attending high school. According to Mrs. B., Alfred's sister came into Alfred's bed one night and touched his genitals. She then asked him to accompany her to the bathroom. Mrs. B. did not know exactly what took place in the bathroom. She was advised by her priest not to discuss the matter with Alfred, because it was the sister who was the aggressor. Mrs. B., however, felt that the incident had a traumatic effect on Alfred. The whereabouts of that sister were unknown to the family during our contact.

Mrs. B. supported the family working as a secretary for the city board of education. The probation officer visited the home, a four-room apartment in a low income housing project. The home was well-kept and comfortable.

Alfred had graduated from one of the best Catholic high schools in. Metropolitan Area in 1966 where both his scholastic work and his behavior were described by a school report as having been good. Alfred had been employed as a mechanic at the Metropolitan Area Telephone Company from August of 1966 to January of 1970. He resigned during the week of his arrest. The employer did not know of the arrest. Alfred was fit for employment. He was in good health (aside from a drug addiction). He had a noticeable limp, as he had been born with one leg shorter than the other.

Regarding the drug use at the time of our contact, Alfred had a heroin habit of $40 to $50 per day. The use of drugs had begun a number of years before when Alfred and his friends were experimenting with various drugs, including marihuana and L.S.D. Alfred advised the probation officer that to support his habit he used his salary ($125 per week) plus overtime pay. He later took out a loan for a car, but used it instead for his habit. He finally sold a car that he had owned, and used that money as well. Alfred admitted that he had occasions to steal small articles, such as a radio, to use the money for drugs; however, he minimized his unlawful means to obtain money for drugs. It was evident that the size of Alfred's habit could not have been supported on his own salary. In March of 1970, immediately following his conviction, Alfred entered a drug treatment program, the Encounter Halfway House. He had made his first contact with them at court and the court had paroled Alfred until his sentencing date (in April of 1970) for him to enter the program. Alfred had been attending the program on a daily outpatient basis. He was in his sixth week of outpatient treatment and was, therefore, eligible to enter their residential program. Alfred's mother wanted him in the program. Alfred told the probation officer that he wanted the residential drug treatment.

Alfred had one prior arrest on April 25, 1968 for grand larceny (auto), driving while intoxicated, leaving the scene of an accident, possession of burglar's tools, and resisting arrest. These charges had been reduced to reckless driving, for which Alfred had been found guilty and given a sentence of $100 fine or thirty days in jail. Alfred explained the charges in the following version: While driving a friend's car (given permission by the friend's mother), Alfred had a minor accident with a car owned by the off-duty arresting officer. In arguing with the officer, Alfred was charged with resisting arrest and leaving the scene. He was charged with grand larceny (auto) and possession of burglar's tools (the car keys), because the owner's father verified that the car was stolen, not knowing that the owner's mother had given Alfred permission to use the car. Alfred advised the probation officer that he had not been intoxicated; and this charge was changed to reckless driving.

With all of the above information known to us, we recommended that Alfred be allowed to continue his already begun drug treatment. We, therefore, recommended that he be placed on probation on the condition that he remain in drug treatment. The court ordered the same.

The case was transferred to another probation officer for supervision, although it was actually the drug program that was supervising Alfred in residence there. After his first three months on probation, Alfred absconded from the drug program. The supervising probation officer was notified and filed a violation of probation. A warrant was issued on the case; and nothing further was heard by our office concerning Alfred. Warrants were not routinely served by Metropolitan Area officials, but were usually served in the course of a subsequent arrest, if one occurred.

Case Analysis of a Robber

The analysis here will be brief, as the P-S process was to operate through a diffused intervention (the residential drug program) and did in fact become interrupted by Alfred's absconsion from the drug program.

Alfred's involvement with drugs could be the focus of the analysis; however, the drug problem and the means which Alfred chose to support his drug habit will be jointly discussed. This was Alfred's first arrest involving violence; however, it was a serious offense. An elderly man was attacked in his own store and quite possibly died as the result of this incident. The reader is probably wondering why the court granted probation in a case of this nature. Before Alfred had been referred to the probation department for the presentence investigation, the court had already positively sanctioned his entrance into the drug program. A recommendation by the probation officer for incarceration for the charge of possession of a hypodermic needle would have been questioned by the court and most probably not followed. (It should be noted that the probation officer did feel that incarceration was appropriate. The case supervisor warned the probation officer of the unlikelihood of the court resorting to incarceration where there was already progress being made through a drug program.) The probation officer's recommendation for probation supervision was, therefore, made reluctantly.

The fact that Alfred absconded from the drug program shortly after being placed on probation indicates that he may have been using the program to avoid incar-

ceration. In cases where drug addicts do not want help
through a drug program, but enter a program on probation supervision, as an alternative to jail, they are
extrinsically motivated to cooperate with the program.
The courts are aware that many drug addicts are not motivated for help with their addiction, but can be extrinsically motivated to enter treatment in lieu of
jail. Under these conditions, the possibility exists
that within time the "unwilling" participant of the
drug program will come to appreciate the program for
itself.

It is, therefore, recognized that probation
supervision combined with drug treatment is seen as the
lesser of two evils by certain drug addicts and that an
unknown percentage of such individuals will come to
benefit intrinsically from their participation in a
program. Because there is no guarantee for this proposed success, perhaps persons who commit violent
crimes to support their drug habit should not be given
this option. It is possible that individuals such as
Alfred should complete the jail time first, and afterwards be offered a drug program to pursue on their own.
However, it must be recalled that, through plea
bargaining (a weakness displayed by the court system),
Alfred's conviction was for a nonviolent crime. The
fact that the complainant had expired appears to have
complicated the case.

Case History of an Assaultist (Repeater)

In July of 1974, Joseph H. (age twenty-five) was
placed on probation for a three-year period for the
charge possession of a dangerous weapon. Specifically,
Joseph and another male companion were walking in
Joseph's neighborhood while intoxicated. According to
Joseph, his companion (the co-defendant) "went wild"
and began breaking windows. The arresting officer apparently saw them from the window of his own apartment
and came on the scene (in civilian clothes, carrying a
gun). A fight ensued between the three. Joseph was
confused as to the identity of the arresting officer
and did not know whether or not he was actually a police officer at the time of the altercation. Joseph
attempted to stab the arresting officer with a knife
that Joseph had been carrying for protection. Another
razor knife was also found in Joseph's possession.
Joseph suffered a broken cheek bone and a subsequent
vision problem. Joseph remained in the City Hospital
for three weeks. He advised the probation officer that

the co-defendant was remanded for mental observation. Joseph acknowledged that he had a past history of assaultive behavior; however, he felt that circumstances in each case warranted a physical altercation.

We ascertained the following personal history during the probation presentence investigation: Joseph was born in Austria and began his early years living in Turkey. He came to the United States at the age of fourteen. Joseph's parents were Crimean. Joseph had been maintaining a very close relationship with his parents. His father (age seventy) was a retired superintendent of an apartment building. His mother (age fifty) was a retired office cleaner. Joseph lost a nineteen-year old brother in 1965 in a canoe drowning; and the parents had lost another son at the age of three in a hospital bombing in Germany. Joseph had one sister (age thirty-three), single, residing in a separate apartment within the same building as Joseph and his parents. The sister was employed as a secretary. Joseph's parents knew nothing about Joseph's prior arrests and learned about the above arrest only because Joseph had been confined to·the hospital with injuries. The parents were under the belief that the above charge had been dismissed. Joseph was residing with his parents, although he was also maintaining another apartment nearby with his girlfriend. The girlfriend was separated from her husband and had one child living with her. Joseph had no plans for marriage.

Joseph had dropped out of high school to work. He was in the army from April of 1968 to April of 1970. His work history after the service had been sporadic. In June of 1973, Joseph's father had retired from his superintendent's job at an eighty-family apartment building. Joseph took over this job, thereby helping his parents retain their apartment rent-free. Joseph began a second job in May of 1974 as an auto mechanic. Although Joseph's parents were receiving pensions and social security benefits, Joseph felt that he was their major source of support.

Joseph had three previous arrests and one arrest subsequent to the present charge, occurring before he was placed on probation. On October 11, 1966, Joseph had been arrested as a passenger on a stolen motorcycle. That case had been dismissed on January 9, 1967. On September 7, 1971, Joseph and friends were arrested for an altercation occurring on a beach in a summer resort area of Metropolitan State. According to

Joseph, the fight was provoked by the other side, who Joseph referred to as "hippies." Joseph admitted that beer drinking had preceded the fight; and Joseph had pulled out a pocket knife during the fight. That case was dismissed on November 23, 1973. On August 14, 1973, Joseph had been arrested (with the same co-defendant as in the present case) on the complaint of a friend. Joseph presented a long and involved story indicating the following: He had taken the complainant's rifle and BB gun out of the complainant's home for the complainant's own safety. As a result, Joseph was arrested with these items in his own home, along with another pistol which Joseph had illegally owned and which he had accidentally discharged in the complainant's home. The charges stemming from that arrest were dismissed on October 4, 1973 and on February 20, 1974. The case which we were investigating had occurred on November 15, 1973; however, while it was still pending, Joseph was arrested again on January 14, 1974. That arrest occurred because of an altercation with the girlfriend's landlord, during which Joseph cut the landlord with a letter opener. The girlfriend changed apartments afterwards and the case was "adjourned in contemplation of dismissal" on June 10, 1974.

In the recommendation within the probation presentence investigation we reminded the court that this was Joseph's first conviction, although he had a history of fighting with weapons. We indicated that it was felt that Joseph was a risk to become involved again in a similar behavior; however, he did verbalize that he would avoid further trouble. Joseph did impress the probation officer as someone wanting to remain in the community so that he could continue to help support his parents. We, therefore, recommended probation supervision coupled with a fine as a reprimand for Joseph's irresponsible behavior. He did receive a fine of $200, which he promptly paid.

The plan for probation supervision included frequent office visits so that we could be a visible reminder to Joseph that he had a great deal to lose by getting involved in fighting again. Joseph took probation supervision seriously, looking upon it as a period of accountability for any of his actions. Joseph reported regularly and called the probation officer when he could not keep an appointment. He was overly polite, usually addressing the probation officer as "ma'am." Joseph was cooperative in reporting trouble.

At an office visit a few months after probation supervision began, Joseph reported that he had lost his
mechanic's job due to a fight. According to Joseph, he
had been provoked into a fight by a co-worker over
whether or not Joseph had been doing his job correctly.
The co-worker alleged that Joseph pulled a knife on
him. Joseph said that this was an inaccuracy that was
reported to the personnel department. Joseph received
a notice from the personnel department advising him
that he was fired due to conduct unbecoming an employee
on the job. Joseph said that he spoke to an executive
at work who believed that Joseph did not have a knife
during the fight and would see to it that the accusa-
tion would be taken off Joseph's employment record.
Joseph was applying for Unemployment Insurance Benefits, but his case was challenged because of the fight.
The probation officer asked Joseph if it would not
embarrass him if a form letter were sent to the personnel department requesting the reason for the firing.
(We were entitled to send the letter, with or without
any probationer's permission; however, it was important
to avoid it if it was felt to be embarrassing.) Joseph
did not object, as he was also curious about how any
future reference from that job would be worded. We received a prompt reply from the personnel department.
(The form had been sent directly to the executive with
whom Joseph had spoken.) There had been a statement
(in the space which asks for the reason for termination) which had been erased. This was noticeable. The
statement that was written over the erasure referred to
a "layoff." Apparently the personnel department decided not to refer to the allegations. Joseph was awaiting a hearing on the Unemployment Insurance Benefits;
however, he did not pursue his application because of
the superintendent's salary that he had been receiving.
It should be noted that Joseph did become concerned
about the fight at work possibly constituting an infraction of his rules of probation supervision. However, as it turned out, there was no official report of
the incident. The fight, therefore, had no bearing on
Joseph's probation case, other than to alert us to the
fact that Joseph was still unable to control his temper. The probation officer, therefore, continued to
discuss this matter with Joseph, advising him that another conviction for assaultive behavior would result
in a loss of probation and a period of confinement.
Joseph was aware of this contingency.

Several months after the above incident, Joseph
reported to the probation officer with a "desk appearance ticket" (notice of arrest and date to appear in

court). The new arrest concerned assaultive behavior
with a neighbor. According to Joseph, he had been an-
noyed by someone making noise that Joseph claimed was
disturbing his girlfriend's child. Joseph went out of
his girlfriend's apartment and had words with the male
neighbor explaining to him that the noise was disturbing the baby's sleep. Joseph could not give the probation officer a clear explanation of why a fight broke
out; nor could he explain why he did not just simply
report the noise to the police. Joseph was worried
about the effect of the new arrest upon his probation
case. The probation officer advised Joseph that a violation of probation would be filed if the new arrest
resulted in a conviction. Joseph then explained his
circumstances to the neighbor, which is felt was a hu-
miliating experience, almost tantamount to begging the
complainant to drop the charges. As it turned out,
Joseph convinced the neighbor that Joseph had a great
deal to lose by a new conviction. The complaint was
dropped. Several months went by uneventfully. Finally, Joseph's case was eligible for early termination
under a new guideline caused by Metropolitan Area's
city budget crisis. According to the guideline, anyone
who had served one year of a three-year probation
period without a new conviction was eligible for early
termination. We submitted Joseph's case to court under
the terms of the new guideline. He was granted an early termination of probation supervision. No progress
report came before the court for scrutiny in these
types of early termination cases. Therefore, the court
had no knowledge of the above two incidents. These incidents only remained reported in our case record,
which was not to be submitted to the court with the
special new forms for early termination. It should be
noted that prior to the city's budget crisis there was
a progress report submitted routinely on any case for
which early termination was being requested. On the
new form there was no need to justify reasons for an
early termination.

The probation officer had no further knowledge of
Joseph's behavior after the last contact with him.

Case Analysis of an Assaultist (Repeater)

Joseph is a habitual personal offender. While he
does not calculate his assaults and pre-plan them, he
continues to settle disputes through assaultive behavior. The behavior is, for the most part, spontaneous.
A situation provokes Joseph, and he resolves the pre-

senting problem through a physical altercation. One would have to know more about the working class, European culture which influenced Joseph's early socialization for one to attribute his behavior to a subculture norm. If, in fact, the peers and adults surrounding Joseph during his early years reinforced "toughness," then Joseph has properly learned from them. The alternate case would be that the early reference groups tried to socialize Joseph into a normative system that opposed fighting; and Joseph failed. If one assumes the former explanation, then there is more hope for redirecting the behavior. If one proceeds to treat Joseph without knowing the specific source of his demonstrated aggressiveness, one must use an external means of control. Perhaps a psychoanalyst could discover the source of the aggressiveness and rely upon an internal mechanism of control to redirect the behavior. The P-S process operating alone had to rely on an external mechanism of socialization.

The probation officer made Joseph aware of the repercussions of further assaultive behavior. Knowing the consequences, Joseph was still unable to refrain from fighting. It is likely that after being placed on probation, Joseph decided to make an effort to abide by the rules of the P-S process. If his masculinity were at stake in an argument, it probably outweighed the consequences of the P-S process. However, if it were only his temper that had to be considered, the consequences of the P-S process probably outweighed the need to act upon provocation.

With a case such as Joseph's, it is difficult to extinguish the undesirable behavior until several applications of punishment are felt by the individual. Joseph's loss of his job (omission) resulted from fighting. One would expect him to not resort to fighting on a future job after this experience. The P-S process was not able to invoke any punishment, as no conviction resulted from the fight at work nor from the subsequent fight with a neighbor. It is not likely that Joseph was able to fully learn from a "close call." He is able to think about how close he came to a violation of probation. However, it is probable that the "scare" was not as potent a reinforcer as would be the actual violation of probation and a period of incarceration. While Joseph recognized the authority of the P-S process, he probably had to experience the punishment before the P-S process would have a successful impact upon him.

One outcome of Joseph's threatened probation status was that he had to apologize to his neighbor, and thereby embarrass himself to avoid prosecution. If manliness was at stake, then Joseph probably had to "lose face" through his plea to his neighbor. Therefore, he met with a punishment (humiliation) only because he had to satisfy the P-S process by not sustaining another conviction. If he were trying to avoid humiliation through fighting, he ironically had to pay the price for it by suffering another form of embarrassment because of his probation status.

Joseph represents an individual who resolves disagreements through physical defense. Although Joseph had been arrested for assaultive behavior several times, he had only been convicted once. Escaping conviction served to reinforce the behavior. Being placed on probation supervision served to caution Joseph that there would be more severe repercussions if he were to sustain another conviction for similar behavior. Joseph showed a complete understanding of the P-S process and of its contingencies. However, under pressure (e.g., being provoked) Joseph resorted to assaultive behavior on two occasions that the probation officer knew of. One instance caused him to lose a job which he had been enjoying. The other instance caused him to be served with a court appearance notice (a re-arrest). If the new arrest had not been dropped by the complainant, and had resulted in a conviction, we would have recommended incarceration. Joseph feared the implementation of that P-S process contingency and intervened by requesting the victim to drop the complaint. In doing so, Joseph suffered embarrassment, an experience which probably was painful to him.

The reader may observe that the P-S process, as a threat, only served to motivate Joseph to use his own resources to "cover up" the behavior which our goal was to prevent. It is likely that although the above description is correct, the incident in its entirety will serve to help deter Joseph from future assaultive behavior. If Joseph went through the "pain" to avoid a violation of probation, it is likely that he will take more concern in the future to avoid the assaultive recourse, and thereby avoid another conviction. (A future conviction would probably result in a jail sentence, because Joseph had already served a period of probation supervision.) It is felt, however, that a period of one year is too brief for probation supervision in Joseph's case. Had it not been for the city's budget crisis, Joseph would have continued under probation supervision. The endurance of abstaining from assaultive behavior would probably have had a long-term effect upon Joseph such that the desired behavior would have continued after termination of a three-year period of probation supervision. Either a revocation of probation (with an accompanying jail term) or a full three-year period of probation supervision would have been more productive in halting assaultive behavior than was the one year of probation supervision.

Case History of an Auto Thief (Repeater)

In August of 1974, Ralph P. (age seventeen) was placed on probation supervision for a three-year period as a "Youthful Offender" for the charge escape, in the third degree. The original charge had been attempted grand larceny, auto. However, Ralph had suffered injuries during an altercation with the complainant and had escaped from hospitalization while under arrest.

According to the probation presentence investigation (received by this probation officer in County B from an investigating probation officer in County A), the following circumstances had led to this arrest: Ralph was attempting to steal an auto, according to the complainant (the car's owner). The complainant interceded whereupon Ralph allegedly tried to stab the complainant with a screw driver. Ralph also struck the arresting officer who had to use force to contain Ralph. Ralph's explanation of the incident, to the investigating probation officer, denied any tampering with the car. According to Ralph, he had been merely leaning on the car, vomiting because he was sick from having been drinking. According to Ralph, the owner of the car struggled with him, stabbing Ralph in the back and leg. While hospitalized, Ralph left; and, therefore, pled guilty to the charge escape.

The probation presentence investigation received by this probation officer presented a very sketchy view of Ralph's personal history. This probation officer had personally conducted two prior presentence reports for Ralph which presented much needed information about him. The brief presentence investigation conducted in County A provided only the following information: Ralph was age seventeen, born in Metropolitan Area, one of four children. He had attended school (County A High School for Boys) until the tenth grade. Previously, Ralph had spent eight months in the State

Training School. He had held employment at a garage and as a cabinet maker. He was currently employed at an automotive supply store, earning $115 per week. The investigating probation officer felt that Ralph had good family ties, including a brother (Pete). The recommendation for probation supervision had been based on the above, plus a prior history with the courts. (There were no other details of personal history or arrest history contained in the report.)

For more background information the reader is referred to the County B probation presentence investigation submitted a year earlier, dated July 3, 1973. The case had concerned a stolen auto which Ralph was found to be driving. The following is the entire personal history and recommendation found in this probation officer's 1973 investigation:

> The def't. is a 16 yr. old, the product of an intact home. The father is a truck driver, the mother is a housewife. There are two sisters, ages 11 and 1 mo., and one older brother. It should be noted that the def't't's. brother has been placed at a juvenile treatment center and is home now planning to enter the marines.
> The def't. dropped out of County A High School in the 9th grade. He had been transferred there from J.H.S. 001 because of an altercation with a teacher.
> The def't. advises us that he is presently employed as a mechanic's helper at G. Service Station (address). We sent a form to the station manager to verify employment; however, the reply has not been received to. date. We asked def't. to bring a letter from his employer to court. The def't. informs us that he has been at his present job for 5 weeks. Previously, he worked for J. Productions for 2-1/2 months (unverified, since def't. could not provide us with an address). The def't. has received counseling from the Court Employment Unit in County C. Crim. Ct., having been referred there from County C Crim. Ct. on his pending charge. His counselor was Ms. W. (phone). We spoke with Ms. W., who informs us that the def't. failed to cooperate with her, would not keep appts., and his case was consequently terminated with

102

the Employment Unit.

Def't. is in good health. He indicates that he had been hospitalized at the
City Hospital and County C. Hospital when
he was younger for psychiatric observation.
We gave the def't. medical release forms to
have mother sign them and return them; however, def't. reported back to us that
mother doesn't feel that the reports would
be relevant.

Def't. admits to a past history of
drug use, i.e., marihuana and heroin. He
claims that he hasn't used heroin for the
past year and that his past use lasted for
3 or 4 mos. Ms. W. of the County C. Crim.
Ct. Employment Unit advises us that she had
arranged for urine analysis on 4/2/73 and
the results were negative.

We had no opportunity to interview
the parents, as mother must remain home
with her 1 month old baby, and father
works. We did have a brief telephone conversation with the mother during which she
indicated that she felt that the week in
jail spent by the def't. on this charge may
have a sobering effect on his future behavior. We learned that the father appears
to be rejecting the def't. because of the
def't's. court involvements.

We spoke to def't's. aftercare worker
from the Metropolitan State Division for
Youth, Mr. D. (phone), who has been supervising the def't. since his release from
the State Training School in 11/72. According to Mr. D., the def't. has reported
only once to Mr. D. and has not kept any
other appts. Mr. D. further advises us
that on the same day that the def't. had
been released from the Training School, he
was arrested for the case now pending in
County C. Crim. Ct. involving the same type
of charge for which he had been sent to the
Training School, which is coincidentally
the same type of charge in this instant offense. Mr. D. advises us that the def't.
is on parole with the Div. for Youth for 2
yrs. as of 11/72; however, in view of
def't's. age, it would be inadvisable for
them to violate him and return him to the
Training School. If the def't. is placed

on probation with us, Mr. D. would continue
to try to work with the def't.

    In view of the above, the def't. ap-
pears to us to be someone who lacks insight
into his behavior and has not in the past
treated his court involvements with any
seriousness. He is obviously attracted to
driving other people's cars, and we don't
know whether he has learned any lessons
about the consequences of such actions.
The mother believes the jail remand has
taught the def't. a lesson. We hope that
this is so. We feel that the def't. does
require supervision and guidance; and we,
therefore, recommend a period of probation
supervision on the conditions that the
def't. cooperate with the Div. for Youth
aftercare worker and cooperate with any
probation referrals for drug treatment if
indicated.

Addendum to Court

    On 5/28/73 the def't. was re-arrested
on a charge of burglary to which def't.
pled guilty on 6/27/73 (docket number, adj.
to 7/10/73, Pt. 3A). We note that our contact with def't. has not had an impact, because he was re-arrested within several
days after an interview with this P.O.
Further, it had been mother's stated opinion that def't. had learned a lesson after
a week spent in remand on this case and
that def't. was not likely to get into further difficulty. Def't. has shown us by
his re-arrest on 5/28 that he is unrespon-
sive to his contacts with this office and
would not be a good candidate for probation
supervision. We are, therefore, changing
our recommendation for probation supervision and are recommending that def't. receive an appropriate jail sentence on this
charge.

    In addition to the aforementioned presentence re-
port, this probation officer submitted another one for
the re-arrest, after having interviewed Ralph and his
new co-defendant in remand (City Correctional Facility). We recommended commitment for both of them.
Therefore, Ralph had a recommendation on both of his

cases for a period of commitment. He received three months for the burglary (shoe store break-in), which was reduced to criminal trespassing and he received six months for the auto charge. However, the court ordered the sentences to run concurrently. Further, although Ralph was eligible for "Youthful Offender" status, the court denied such status, and the charges stood as such (unauthorized use of a motor vehicle and criminal trespassing).

With the above information known, on August 7, 1974, this probation officer met with Ralph for his first probation-supervision appointment (which he was serving for his most recent County A arrest). It was learned that Ralph had been unemployed for one and a half months, because of his arrest. However, he had confidence that he could get another auto mechanic job. It was agreed that getting another job was something that the probation officer felt him capable of doing. It was also expressed to him that the probation officer was quite surprised to have found him placed on probation because it was not felt that he could comply with the rules. He explained that he intended to keep appointments with the probation officer and to cooperate. At this point the probation officer let Ralph know that the probation officer had no faith in Ralph's ability to stay away from other people's cars. Ralph told the probation officer to watch and see that he can manage to stay away from stolen cars. The probation officer and Ralph challenged each other (without actually "betting" anything). Each "bet" the other that the other would be proved wrong. The probation officer did advise Ralph that the most sensible thing to do was to work and save money to buy a car of his own. He agreed. The plan for supervision was to keep Ralph "challenged" to keep his "bet" that he would not steal another car.

Ralph was unable to keep his next appointment two weeks later because by August 23, 1974 he was already re-arrested (in our County B) concerning a stolen car. Ralph's mother had called to tell the probation officer that Ralph was in remand at City Correctional Facility. We then received his re-arrest as a new probation presentence investigation to be completed, as he had pled guilty to the charge attempted unauthorized use of a motor vehicle. The probation officer interviewed Ralph in remand. Ralph admitted that he had been a passenger in a stolen car with two others. Ralph advised the probation officer that his nineteen-year old brother, Peter (a co-defendant), had stolen the car and was doing the driving. Ralph claimed that, at the time of his arrest, he was too intoxicated on wine to realize the consequences of his actions.

During the above interview, Ralph told the probation officer that he had a religious-like inspiration to stay out of trouble in the future. The probation officer told Ralph that we could guarantee that behavior for a few months, as the probation officer advised him that we were recommending a commitment on this new arrest. Ralph was advised that the probation officer would try to recommend to the County A court that he not "do time" on the violation of probation which had to be filed there. Ralph provided a new piece of information for his background to be presented to the court. He advised the probation officer (as did his mother) that he had a girlfriend due to give birth four months later. There were no plans for marriage, although they had recently been living together a few months before. (It should be noted that in the presentence report prepared by this probation officer in July of 1973 for the shoe store break-in, the same type of information was offered as a reason for Ralph's felt need to remain in the community.) At that time he advised the probation officer that he had a fifteen-year old girlfriend due to give birth to a child that Ralph wanted to support. At that time, the probation officer knew his girlfriend's name, since the girlfriend's brother was a co-defendant in the auto which Ralph had been driving in our very first case with Ralph. It was not clear whether Ralph was still referring to the same girlfriend in August of 1974. In any event, too many other circumstances in Ralph's case overshadowed any consideration of his expected putative fatherhood.

Ralph received a three-month period of confinement on the August, 1974 arrest, as per our recommendation. We filed a violation of probation in County A Criminal Court based on the new County B conviction. We advised the court that Ralph was in City Correctional Facility; and we, therefore, asked that a warrant be lodged with the Department of Corrections for Ralph to be brought from City Correctional Facility to County A Criminal Court for a hearing on the violation of probation. We recommended that if the violation were upheld, the case be adjourned for several weeks for a progress report on Ralph's community adjustment after his release from incarceration. It is not known why Ralph was released directly from City Correctional Facility to return home. (Perhaps the paperwork was slow in getting to the proper person.) Ralph had been released early for time credited to him while he was in remand. Therefore, he was back home, with no appearance made in County A Criminal Court. The probation officer received a phone call from Ralph's mother questioning a notification mailed to him by County A Criminal Court. The probation officer explained everything to Mrs. P. for her to relate to Ralph. Mrs. P. was advised that there was now a bench warrant issued in County A Criminal Court, requiring Ralph to present himself there. Mrs. P. informed the probation officer that Ralph had started a new job and was too busy to go to court. The probation officer advised Mrs. P. that if Ralph did not go to court, some day when he least expected it, warrant officers would pick him up at home. The probation officer further advised Mrs. P. that although Ralph could receive up to one year's period of incarceration on the violation of probation, we were not recommending confinement yet. Mrs. P. was advised that Ralph could possibly complete the remainder of his three-year probation period.

As it turned out, Ralph did not willingly present himself in County A Criminal Court. Instead, he was in County B Supreme Court in February of 1975, arrested for a burglary charge. The new charge was pending for a couple of months. In the interim, no action was taken on the County A violation of probation, as that court was awaiting our addendum of the outcome of the newest case. We followed the court actions on the new case which finally resulted in a conviction and a County B Supreme Court probation presentence investigation (to be conducted by a probation officer assigned to that court). In the interim, a drug program representative interviewed Ralph in remand and convinced Ralph to join the program as a resident in their therapeutic community. The program representative and Ralph called this probation officer reporting that there had been a current heroin addiction for which Ralph was motivated to get treatment. We felt this to be a ploy of Ralph's to avoid jail time. We considered Ralph to be more suited for the state's own drug program. However, it was arranged through County B Supreme Court and the drug program to parole Ralph to the therapeutic community. The investigating probation officer in County B Supreme Court recommended probation supervision on the condition that Ralph cooperate with the drug program with which he was already in residence. The court ordered the above and Ralph received a County B Supreme Court supervision probation officer for a five-year period beginning in May of 1975. This probation offi-

cer spoke with the new probation officer and then reported back to County A in an addendum to the violation
of the three-year criminal court probation case. Because no one serves two probation cases at the same
time and because Ralph was now on probation to a higher
court, we recommended a withdrawal of our violation of
probation and a termination of probation supervision on
our case. The court ordered the same; and this probation officer had no further contacts with Ralph.

Case Analysis of an Auto Thief (Repeater)

Ralph represents a habitual property offender,
perhaps on his way toward becoming a "career criminal."
He is not a good candidate for the P-S process, as he
cannot even spend time involved in opportunistic
learning. The accumulation of arrests that Ralph had
experienced in such a short period of time indicates
that his periods of confinement, youth parole, and probation contacts did little to deter him from continuing
his offenses.

While a probation officer must guard himself/her-
self against making premature predictions to a probationer of expectations for his/her failure, this probation officer made such a prophecy in Ralph's case. It
is recognized that this probation officer may have
aborted Ralph's success, through a self-fulfilling prophecy. However, Ralph had already proved his failure
to this probation officer in more ways than one. If he
had been sincere in promising a change in behavior,
then the disbelief expressed to him should have served
as a challenge to him to disprove.

We did exercise the ultimate, negative reinforcer
of the P-S process, the violation of probation. However, because we had recommended incarceration on the
re-arrest, we allowed for particularistic treatment upon a finding of guilt on the violation. We had recommended a period of assessment of Ralph's progress in
the community, before a court decision on resentencing.
Had the Supreme Court re-arrest not occurred, it is
likely that we would have recommended restoration to
probation. However, it is felt that Ralph would probably have been arrested again. For the perplexed
reader who wonders why the P-S process allows someone
like Ralph to have another chance at probation, the answer is uncomplicated. Ralph may have been living an
adult's life, but he was still young and entitled to
another chance (especially because his offenses were

not of a violent nature). But with another opportunity on probation supervision, if Ralph had failed, it is likely that he would never be granted probation supervision again.

Any reformative outcome in Ralph's case would not likely be brought about under probation supervision. The reform for Ralph, if it ever does occur, will result when Ralph has had enough jail time and wants no more.

Case History of a White-Collar Criminal (Employee Theft)

In June of 1974, Alice C. (age eighteen) was placed on probation for a three-year period as a "Youthful Offender" for the charge petit larceny. Specifically, Alice was charged with taking items and money from her employer, a chain drug store. Alice admitted that, while she was employed as a cashier at the drug store for several months, she had been taking items home without paying for them, e.g., radio, other small electrical appliances, a wrist watch, etc. She claimed that everyone else was doing it; and the opportunity was there. She also admitted to having taken money occasionally from the cash register till; however, she claimed that the amounts were small and probably added up to $50 over a period of several months. Alice advised the probation officer that there was no need for her to have extra money, as she had been working at the job part-time while in school. Her family, with whom she had been living, provided well for her. She regretted having committed the offense, due to the embarrassment and financial loss (attorney fees) that her family had suffered. Alice had been apprehended by an undercover security guard employed by the drug firm. Alice later found out that other salesclerks had been caught, including a girl who had suggested the pilferage to Alice. Alice was disturbed about the fact that she had signed a confession for the security guard on the promise that Alice's parents would not be notified and that the store would not press charges. The confession named an arbitrary total amount of theft at $1,000. Alice did not realize the importance of that figure until the security guard advised her that after criminal court, she would be faced with a civil suit, requesting repayment. Alice advised the probation officer that she returned the items that she had previously taken home. Additionally, the store took approximately $50 in cash from her last two paychecks. When the probation officer spoke to Alice's parents, who accompanied her to the office, they seemed to have recovered from the embarrassment and were more concerned with affirming that Alice was a "good girl." Her mother may have been aware of Alice's pilferage, as the mother had accepted a wrist watch from Alice without asking any serious questions. The mother also felt terrible that Alice had been caught when one considers that "everyone else was doing it."

Through Alice and her parents we gathered the following personal history for Alice: Alice was the product of an intact home wherein she had a younger brother (age eleven). The father was employed for the city as a sanitation worker. He had been on the job close to the retirement period, although he appeared to be younger than his stated age. The mother was a housewife. Alice had an average school record and discontinued school in her senior year. Her grandmother had paid for some supplementary clerical schooling for Alice. There was no reported drug use; and Alice was in good health. After Alice was fired from her part-time job at the drug store, she found a full-time clerical job which she liked. There was no prior arrest record for Alice.

With the above information known, we recommended probation supervision in order to follow up on any future financial problem or a present one that might have been withheld from the probation officer. The court ordered the same.

Under probation supervision, Alice reported regularly after work once every month. (Her boyfriend sometimes accompanied her, waiting in the reception area for her.) She showed the probation officer all of her pay stubs. She received a raise and a vacation, and continued to enjoy her employment. There were no reported problems at home. Alice was very upset about the fact that the store followed through on their civil court suit against her. The store was awarded restitution in the amount of $1,000. Alice's concern was over the fact that the figure was exaggerated and that she had been "railroaded" into signing the original confession. Alice showed the probation officer receipts for regular payments of $60 per month that she had been making to her former employer. Eventually, Alice was able to start a savings account, but the payments to the former employer were felt by her.

After one year of the three-year probation period had passed uneventfully, we considered the case for early termination of probation. We submitted a complete progress report to the court, including copies of payments being made through the civil court case. We asked for probation to be terminated early as improved in July of 1975. The court ordered the same. This probation officer had no further contacts with Alice.

Case Analysis of a White-Collar Criminal
(Employee Theft)

Alice represents an individual who used a seemingly low-risk situation to prosper at the expense of her employer. One motivation for Alice's theft was that her co-workers seemed to be using their positions to take merchandise and money without being detected. Alice did not appear to have had any inhibitions preventing her from committing an employee theft. She had not expressed to the probation officer any feelings about her actions having been inherently wrong. Her remorse stemmed from the consequences that she had experienced through civil court and the criminal processing.

In this particular case, the P-S process was the least concern to Alice when compared to the other consequences that she suffered as a result of her theft. The unexpected apprehension, the humiliation, her parents' costs, and her civil court restitution were more psychologically and monetarily damaging to Alice than was the probation-supervision status. Further, these other consequences that had been experienced served to deter Alice from repeating the offense. Probation supervision functioned to monitor Alice's behavior afterwards, particularly her employment and her budgeting. Alice was exemplary in following her conditions of probation. Perhaps she might not have taken the P-S process seriously had it not been for all of the outside consequences that befell her.

As a result of Alice's cooperation with us, we removed the probation-supervision status earlier than scheduled, under favorable conditions (as "negative reinforcement"). It was the probation officer's impression that Alice had learned a lesson from her apprehension. The lesson is that "crime does not pay." It is not likely that she learned that white-collar crime is wrong, because evidence exists all around her in the larger society that everyone (especially those in high positions) are eluding detection and prosecution or are

111

receiving mild punishments. Norms regarding white-collar crime are confusing to the average citizen. In such an anomic situation propriate learning would be difficult. Alice's case may serve as an example that perhaps strict enforcement of white-collar offenses at all levels of society would cause others to abstain through opportunistic learning.

Case History of a Drug Addict 1

In June of 1974, Frank D. (age twenty-seven) was placed on probation for a three-year period for the charge criminal possession of drug paraphernalia. The special condition of probation supervision stated that Frank was to cooperate with the New Directions drug program. (Frank had already entered the above-mentioned residential therapeutic community during the presentence investigation.)

The presentence investigation (which had been conducted by another probation officer) revealed the following: While under the influence of drugs, Frank had entered into an altercation with three other males. Frank called the police for assistance and apparently identified himself as a police officer. When the police arrived and eventually searched Frank, they found drug paraphernalia on him, as well as a gun holster. Frank explained to the probation department that earlier that day he had loaned his gun (forty-one Magnum, unregistered) to a friend; and he still had the holster with him.

The following personal history was also found in the probation presentence report. Frank's parents were divorced when he was four years old. His father died (homicide) in January of 1974. (Nothing more specific was said in the report about the father's death.) Frank had graduated from an out-of-state air academy in 1965 and shortly afterwards joined the military. He was honorably discharged in 1968. Frank had held employment usually as a waiter or a chef. He began drug use in the military. Frank's most recent addiction was on methadone at $16 to $30 per day. He detoxified in the County C House of Detention after his arrest and was receptive to a contact with the New Directions drug program. Frank stated to the investigating probation officer that he was aware of his need for help in drug abstinence. He referred to a prior frightening incident wherein he was once pronounced "dead on arrival" at a hospital following an overdose. A prior arrest (the only other arrest for Frank) in October of 1971, involved assaultive behavior (possibly while under the influence of drugs). That case resulted in a conviction and conditional discharge.

Prior to the current charge, Frank had been unemployed and living with his mother who was employed as a secretary. Mrs. D. became actively involved in the parents' group at New Directions.

Because Frank was a resident of a drug program, the probation-supervision function consisted of maintaining contact with the program and receiving progress reports. Office visits to the probation officer were not required in these types of cases. This probation officer routinely held one initial interview with this type of probationer for introduction purposes and to explain the conditions of probation. Therefore, such an appointment was arranged with Frank. Oddly enough, he did not come with an escort. It became clearer to this probation officer after conversation that Frank had made steady progress with the program, earning responsibility with the progress. He seemed engrossed in the hierarchy within the program, with hopes to rise to staff responsibilities.

Several months after the contact with Frank, the probation officer was contacted by Frank, Mrs. D., and the director of the drug program. The problem was that Frank had left the program. All the written progress reports that we had been receiving were favorable. Regression to drug use was not the source of the problem. The program sent a representative to talk to the probation officer about their version of why Frank had left the program. The program representative was very vague about Frank's reasons. He felt that Frank could not accept his limitations. It was his view that Frank was a perfectionist who had put a great deal of effort into helping the program grow, e.g., soliciting funds for it, keeping stray members from leaving, etc. Then it appeared that Frank was setting goals too high for himself and withdrew when he could do no more. This explanation resembled one that a trained psychologist would have constructed. The explanation was accepted, because the program had known Frank as a resident for eight months. We were asked by the program to enforce the condition of probation that he cooperate with their program. The probation officer did not promise to do that; but we did assure the program that we would try to motivate Frank to return. The probation officer then saw Frank in the office. His mother had called before the visit and arranged to see the probation officer after Frank. She did not want Frank to think that she was "meddling." She, therefore, asked the probation officer not to tell Frank of her appointment. She made it clear that she was interested in helping, not in "taking sides." She did not know whether Frank was right or whether the program was right; but she wanted the probation officer to determine that. When Frank came to the office, he explained why he had left the program. To him, it looked as though he had reached a climax in helping the program. Perhaps he had worked too fast, but he lost an incentive to continue in the program. Further, Frank was concerned about the fact that he was over twenty-seven years old and had no intimate social life. He felt that the program was geared to persons younger than he; and that most of the others were probably not in a position to feel the deprivation of a social life that he was experiencing. Frank had been home from the program for a few days and had no thoughts about returning to drug use. He did go out drinking one night, but had not overdone it. Frank intended to look for work and stay with his mother until he could afford his own apartment.

We had an obligation to enforce the condition of probation requiring that Frank cooperate with the drug program. However, it was felt that the probation officer could use discretion in this matter and allow Frank a period in which to assess his progress. The probation officer did try to motivate Frank to return to the program. Frank was told that the program cared a great deal about him. He agreed that they did; but he also felt that if the program could bring him back they would win the confidence of a lot of peripheral members. If the program could not bring Frank back they would "lose face" to all members. Frank felt that he was now a symbol to the program. He felt that, if they really cared enough about him, they would let him try to make it on his own. He was willing to go to evening meetings and be a member of the program, but not a resident. He was glad that his mother was maintaining her membership with the program's parents' group. The probation officer reminded Frank that his orders of probation had to be enforced with regard to the clause which specified his cooperation with the drug program. Frank advised the probation officer that he was willing to appear in court on a violation of probation. He indicated that he would rather face a jail term than be put back in the program. We were very much aware of the way in which the court would view the proposed violation of probation. It was felt that the court would find guilt (probably through a simple admission by Frank or through a report from the program). However, it was felt that the court would allow Frank to continue on probation with a modification of his orders of probation. The probation officer was in a position to anticipate the court's view better than Frank could and better than the program could. Frank seemed to honestly believe that he could go to jail if he did not return to the program. The program felt that the court would order Frank back to the program. The probation officer conferred with the case supervisor asking whether we had to file a violation or whether we could hold the special condition of probation in abeyance. The supervisor advised that we could do the latter, but that we should see to it that Frank was receiving some auxiliary service such as urine analysis, etc. from another drug program. In the interim, Frank was advised to go about his business of looking for a job until we made a final decision. (The probation officer had wanted to speak to Frank's mother first.) In conversing with Frank, it was noticed that he was very open about his personal feelings. We felt that he would be amenable to psychotherapy on a one-to-one basis. He was asked whether he would consider a referral to a male, psychiatric social worker who the probation officer knew to be very concerned about clients. Frank became very interested in the suggestion and was left with that thought in mind.

The probation officer then saw Mrs. D. and advised her of all of the findings and interpretations. (None of the conversation with Frank was of a "confidential" nature; and, therefore, it could be shared with his mother.) Mrs. D. verified that Frank had been doing well at home for the past few days. Mrs. D. worked as a secretary and was able to support Frank until he could begin work. She was very willing to have him at her home until he would be ready to get his own apartment. Mrs. D. was somewhat concerned about her position with the drug program. She felt pressured in that she would be interacting with the program and would probably have to account for her failure to help get Frank back into the program. Mrs. D. was, nevertheless, not applying any pressure to Frank.

The probation officer spoke to the psychiatric social worker, Mr. S., who maintained an office next door to the probation department. (We had an agreement with his agency, the local State Hospital outpatient clinic, to refer clients there free of charge, in return for our free office space provided for the clinic.) Mr. S. accepted the case after hearing the background, and set up an appointment for Frank.

In the interim, the program had learned, through Frank, Mrs. D., and another contact with us, that we had chosen the above plan. The director of the program, Mr. P., and the program's representative, Mr. R., (who had seen the probation officer) requested that the case be returned to court for a violation of probation. The probation officer advised them that the probation department was the only agency able to request that the case be "calendared" for that reason--and we were not arranging a calendaring of the case. A few minutes later, the case supervisor received the same type of call from the program. The supervisor, having already discussed the case with the probation officer, supported the probation officer's position on the case. Then the program called again advising us that they could accept Frank back as a nonresident member. They also provided a plan of therapy on an arrangement between their program and the nearby hospital. The probation officer now saw Frank's point about the program needing Frank back to "save face." We advised the program that their new plan merely duplicated our proposed plan. They were advised that we would seek their services if Frank regressed on our plan.

The probation officer began seeing Frank regularly and verifying with Mr. S. that therapy appointments were going well. Collateral contacts with Mrs. D. were held; and she was also in contact with the therapist. Frank held good-paying jobs as a cook in more than one place for a few months at a time. For several weeks, Frank was out of work and spent time helping a friend renovate her bar/discoteque. Then Frank was given an offer from the friend to rent the premises and run the bar. Frank was very enthusiastic and discussed his plans with the probation officer. Frank felt that he could make the bar solvent if he turned it into a gay bar. He began pursuing these ends. When he was ready to close the deal to take over the bar, the owner had a better offer from someone with money. (Frank did not have money, but was going to be paying rent from the expected profit.) Frank was very disappointed, as he had envisioned himself the manager of a profitable business. At the same time Mr. S., who had a very good rapport with Frank, motivated him to apply to a community college to study hotel management and culinary arts. Frank's application to school was delayed when the school advised him to retake the general equivalency diploma test, as his scores from several years ago were too low. Frank made plans to retake the test, but then changed his mind in favor of working long hours as a cook to accumulate money. For the next couple of weeks, Frank missed several appointments with Mr. S. because of work and forgetfulness. Mr. S. was going to terminate Frank's case, but Frank asked him not to do so. Frank had initially begun unburdening himself to Mr. S. in sessions during which Frank had been known to cry. It was undoubtedly a very strong therapeutic relationship; however, Frank was less dependent upon it after awhile.

In June of 1975, Frank came to the office and introduced the probation officer to his wife of three days, Pat. This was very unexpected as Frank had not mentioned a close girlfriend beforehand. Frank explained that he had known Pat from the neighborhood for several years. Apparently she discontinued a relationship with a recent boyfriend and became closer to Frank. Frank and Pat were talking about getting married one night when they decided to spontaneously do it. Pat had been working as a secretary and was going to continue her job. Frank was working long hours as a cook. They showed the probation officer the lease to their new apartment; and a visit for August of 1975 was arranged.

At the visit to Frank and Pat's apartment in August of 1975, the probation officer found it to be a new apartment building in a quiet, residential section. The interior of the apartment was expensively, although not completely, furnished. They were buying very expensive furniture and slowly finishing one room at a time. In the probation officer's opinion, Frank was thoroughly occupied with his job, his wife and his new apartment. This was a good position for him to be in, as his case was eligible for early termination under the city's new budget crisis guidelines. Frank had completed one year of his three-year supervision period without a new conviction. That, in itself, made the case eligible for termination. In the probation officer's view, it was not seen how we could be of further service to Frank. There did not appear to be any regression to drug use. Frank continued to see his therapist, although sporadically. There were no presenting problems in the case. We submitted the case to court for early termination, which the court ordered.

This probation officer had no further contacts with Frank after August of 1975, although Mr. S. continued to see him.

Case Analysis of a Drug Addict 1

Frank had a physical dependence on methadone when he came to the attention of the court, and he had used various other drugs in the past for the promotion of euphoria. There are basically two broad approaches to the treatment of drug addicts. One approach is methadone maintenance, a pharmacological form of treatment for heroin addicts. Another approach is through a therapeutic community, based on peer self-help. Because Frank was not addicted to heroin and was amenable to a peer self-help program, he entered such a program as a resident. The program that Frank entered, New Directions, based its treatment upon behavior modification techniques, e.g., rewards of promotion in job status, punishments of degradation ceremonies, etc. The aim of the program was essentially to teach self-discipline, which in turn would lead to drug abstinence, as well as lead to facing up to responsibilities.

Because Frank remained in the program successfully for eight months, it would appear that he found the program meaningful. The program was geared to a residential stay of approximately eighteen months. Frank felt that he had accomplished all that he could through the program in eight months. He also found that the program was stifling his social life. There had been no sign of drug use by Frank since his entrance into the program. With all of these factors taken into account, the probation department had a decision to make as to whether we would insist on Frank's continuance in the program, or allow him to return home.

The P-S process does repay successful adjustment on probation by recommending an early termination of probation. The same negative reinforcement applies to a successful performance in a drug program. While we do not encourage probationers to leave drug programs prematurely, we can evaluate a request to discontinue with a program. In a sense, our decision to allow Frank to leave the program could be viewed in part as a reward for his cooperation shown. A more important reason for our decision had to do with whether our negative reinforcer could motivate Frank to continue. The probation officer did remind Frank that he could

face a violation of probation if he left the drug program. His response to this "threat" was that he would
accept the punishment if it came about. Rather than
force the issue, it was the probation department's
judgment to grant permission to Frank to return home
and to supplement the supervision with psychotherapy.
When such discretion is used by the P-S process, it illustrates our flexibility or our allowance of particularism.

Our decision in Frank's case was not proved wrong
by Frank's subsequent behavior. He was able to abstain
from drugs (to the best of our knowledge), maintain employment, begin a marriage, and avoid further contacts
with the law. We requested early termination of his
case (due to budget considerations). The departmental
directive required us to terminate cases where no conviction had occurred after the first of three years of
probation supervision. Had it not been for this directive, we would have continued to supervise Frank's case
because of the likelihood of relapse among former drug
addicts. A year's supervision is not an accurate gauge
to measure lasting successful behavioral change. We do
not know for what length of time, after this probation
officer's last contact, Frank has been able to abstain
from drugs.

Case History of a Drug Addict 2

In June of 1970, Joyce F. (age twenty) was placed
on probation for a three-year period for the charge
criminal possession of a forged instrument. Specifically, Joyce and two companions (one male and one female) were stopped by police while the girls had in
their possession two stolen social security checks.
Joyce claimed that she and the other girl had found the
checks in an envelope on the ground. She admitted that
they each forged a check and then, on the advice of the
male companion, were on their way to cash the checks.
Joyce denied breaking into the complainant's mailbox
which was located in the same apartment building in
which Joyce's female co-defendant lived. The complainants were an elderly couple living within the same
low-income housing project in which Joyce lived. The
amounts of the checks were $39.40 and $10.20.

Joyce denied current usage of drugs. She admitted she had used heroin for a two-month period at the
age of fifteen. In discussing a previous arrest for
Joyce (that had occurred in October of 1969), the pro-

bation officer confronted Joyce with the arresting officer's written report at that time which indicated that he had checked off items which had led him to observe that Joyce had appeared to be under the influence of drugs. Joyce denied the officer's observations. Concerning that previous arrest (the only other arrest for Joyce), it occurred on October 11, 1969 for petit larceny and criminal possession of stolen property. Joyce explained that she and two others were in a department store when Joyce shoplifted a knit suit. Her only excuse for the offense was that the suit had cost $100; and Joyce had only $50 with her. This case was to be dismissed upon sentencing in the current case.

The following personal history was ascertained during the probation presentence investigation: Joyce was the product of a broken home wherein she had two siblings and two half-siblings. Joyce's father left home in 1955; and Mrs. F. obtained an Enoch Arden decree (awarding a divorce due to a seven year absence) out of state in 1962. Mr. F.'s whereabouts have been unknown since the time he had left the home. Joyce had an older brother, age twenty-two, who had been convicted of armed robbery in 1967 and had very recently received a dismissal in a case concerning possession of a hypodermic needle. Joyce had a younger sister, age eighteen, married. Joyce had two half-siblings, ages seven and fourteen who had been born out-of-wedlock. Mrs. F. had hoped to marry the father of these two children, but Joyce and her brother protested. He married someone else, but remained in close contact with Mrs. F.'s younger children.

The probation officer found Mrs. F. to be a very concerned parent. A visit to the home showed it to be a very clean five-room apartment in a low-income housing project. The Department of Social Services supported the family.

Joyce had graduated from high school with above average grades in June of 1968. She had been employed as a nurse's aid from September of 1968 to November of 1969. The probation officer's first contact with Joyce was in May of 1970 and she had been still unemployed, idle, and receiving spending money from her mother.

We recommended probation supervision for Joyce; and her case was transferred to another probation officer. It was not until two years later in July of 1972 that the case was transferred back to this probation officer to continue with the remainder of Joyce's supervision. For those first two years in which this probation officer had no contact with Joyce, the written record of supervision is relied upon, and it reveals the following:

At the first office visit with her new probation officer on June 25, 1970, Joyce tearfully admitted that she was addicted to heroin and needed help in detoxifying. She did not make this known during the probation investigation because she felt that it would lead to a sentence of commitment to the state narcotics addiction program. (That particular program, which has since been revised, had a very poor reputation among drug addicts.) Joyce's admitted heroin habit had begun sporadically in May of 1967 and had risen in June of 1970 to six to eight bags per day. The former probation officer referred Joyce to a local hospital where Joyce stayed from July 2, 1970 to July 30, 1970 for detoxification. Before her admission, Joyce had talked about follow-up at the New Dimensions therapeutic community; however, upon her release from the hospital, she decided to live with a married, female friend in another neighborhood. The plan was to stay away from the housing project. In November of 1970, Joyce returned to her mother's home in the housing project. That same month, Mrs. F. called the former probation officer and reported that Joyce had used drugs over the weekend. Joyce was seen by that probation officer on the same date of her mother's contact. A referral was made to the Neighborhood Narcotics Counseling Center. They, in turn, referred Joyce to the New Dimensions program for a residential, therapeutic-community treatment program. The probation department then maintained supervision by receiving written monthly progress reports from the program.

On August 9, 1971 the former probation officer received a letter from New Dimensions advising that Joyce had dropped out of their program without their approval on July 9, 1971. (It is not known why it took one month to notify the probation department.) Joyce was seen every few days by the former probation officer until she could decide upon whether or not to return to New Dimensions. She expressed a fondness for the other residents but a fear of the staff. She was upset at the staff for having demoted her from one job to a lower-level one. The reason for the staff action was the fact that Joyce would not "open up" during encounter sessions. The former probation officer had sensed that Joyce feared verbal openness with the group. After much hesitance, Joyce agreed to return to the Neighborhood Narcotics Counseling Center (the original program), but she only went on two occasions and could not be motivated to continue.

Joyce began to miss appointments in October and November of 1971. When the former probation officer visited the home in November of 1971, it was learned that Joyce was pregnant. The father of the child was reported to be the brother of the woman that Joyce had been staying with previously. There were no plans to marry. The former probation officer noted a severe despondency on the part of Joyce during the pregnancy. Joyce would not keep probation appointments nor go anywhere except for prenatal appointments. Although the despondency was noticeable, there were no indications of drug use.

In April of 1972, Joyce gave birth to a baby girl. The former probation officer visited the home in May of 1972 and felt that Joyce was in better spirits after the baby's birth. Joyce was remaining in her mother's home with the baby. At this time the former probation officer was taking a leave of absence and explained to Joyce that the case was being transferred back to the probation officer who had done the investigation.

This probation officer received transfer of the case in July of 1972. After an initial office interview, this probation officer decided to supervise through home visits. Joyce was told that we were doing so for her convenience because of the infant. This was partially true; but the main reason that the probation officer wanted to make home visits was to see the kind of care that the baby was receiving and also to make the probation officer more available to Mrs. F. who had been reliable about reporting Joyce's drug use in the past.

For several months, home visits indicated no problems. Joyce's married sister was in the home during one of the visits. She was separated from her husband. The sister and Joyce were looking for an apartment to share. Joyce wanted to work and have her sister mind her child (as well as the sister's own children). The plan was feasible, but the probation officer was concerned about Joyce leaving her mother's supervision. We let Joyce plan for the change, but

122

fortunately she made no progress in finding an apartment.

On February 1, 1973, Mrs. F. called in a very upset state of mind. She reported that she had found hypodermic needles and syringes in Joyce's belongings.
Mrs. F. also observed signs of regression in Joyce,
e.g., late hours, staying away from home for days at a
time and borrowing money from Mrs. F. without repaying
it. (Joyce was at this time receiving Department of
Social Service Aid to Dependent Children expenses for
her and the baby.) Mrs. F. was told to have Joyce report to the office on the following day. Since Mrs. F.
had thrown away the drug paraphernalia, the probation
officer advised her to save the next "set of works"
that might be found and report it to police. Joyce
failed to report on the next day; nor was she available
for the next two immediate appointments. On February
7, 1973, Joyce answered the telephone when the probation officer called the home. She admitted that her
mother had found the drug paraphernalia; however, Joyce
claimed that she had been holding it for someone else.
Joyce denied drug use and claimed that there was no
need for her to re-enter drug treatment. Joyce was
given an appointment for later that day, but she failed
to keep it. She failed to keep the next appointment,
as well.

On February 15, 1973, the probation officer
visited the home. Mrs. F. was there alone. She presented two hypodermic needles, syringes, a bottle cap,
a thin piece of tubing, and a bobby pin--all of which
she reported finding under Joyce's bed mattress and in
Joyce's housecoat. Mrs. F. was asked to call the police to present the above to them and to file a complaint regarding the items. When the police arrived,
they discussed the matter with Mrs. F. and with the
probation officer. The police advised the probation
officer that they did not have grounds for a complaint
against Joyce. In fact, they said that if they had to
make an arrest, they would have to arrest Mrs. F. since
the drug paraphernalia was in her possession. (The
logic of the police officers evaded the probation officer, who had seen a similar situation result in an arrest on another case.) The police offered to voucher
the drug paraphernalia at the precinct so that we could
refer to it as evidence in a violation of probation.
The probation officer accompanied the police to the
precinct and received a receipt and voucher number for
the items. Joyce failed to keep an appointment on the
following day. She refused to come to the telephone to

speak to the probation officer on February 16, 1973. On that same date we prepared a violation of probation. The grounds for the violation included: (1) Joyce's failure to keep appointments, (2) Joyce's "failure to obey such other instruction of the probation officer as may be imposed to insure compliance with the conditions of probation," and (3) Joyce's failure to associate only with law-abiding persons and maintain reasonable hours. (It should be noted that item number two in the violation of probation is a "catchall" phrase and stated condition of probation. It allows us to make a justifiable request of the probationer, which must be complied with.) On February 22, 1973, the violation of probation was presented to the court. On that date a "declaration of delinquency" was declared. (This court action guards against the probation period expiring while the court decides on the matter.) The case was adjourned until March 12, 1973, with notice sent to Joyce to appear in court on that date. On March 12, 1973, Joyce failed to appear; and a bench warrant was, therefore, issued. Mrs. F. was advised to call the warrant officer (or local precinct) to serve the warrant when Joyce was in the house. Mrs. F. was also advised that if the baby were in Joyce's care, we would have to notify the Bureau of Child Welfare for Child Neglect proceedings. At that time the baby, however, was with Mrs. F. and she was not going to permit Joyce to take the infant out of the home.

The warrant remained unserved for several months. On June 7, 1973, Joyce appeared before the court and the bench warrant was vacated. The case was adjourned until June 21, 1973. (It should be noted that the case was originally due to be terminated in June of 1973, as a three-year probation period.) On June 21, 1973, Joyce entered a plea of not guilty. The case was adjourned until July 12, 1973 at which time Joyce changed her plea to guilty. The case was adjourned to August 16, 1973 for a recommendation from the probation officer for sentencing. On August 16, 1973, Joyce failed to appear; and a bench warrant was issued. Joyce later found out that we were recommending the termination of probation supervision; and she finally appeared in court on September 20, 1973. We had based the recommendation on several contacts with Joyce in July and August of 1973. She denied drug use and was not motivated to re-enter drug treatment although she reported to the Neighborhood Narcotics Counseling Center once in July of 1973. She claimed that the drug paraphernalia found in February of 1973 was left at the home by a

friend. In August of 1973, Mrs. F. felt that Joyce had
been functioning well and that there were no signs of
drug use. We apprised the court that we had given our
maximum efforts to Joyce over a period of three years
and could do no further for her. It is unclear as to
why the court did not simply terminate the case.
Instead of a simple termination, on September 20, 1973,
the presiding judge revoked probation and resentenced
Joyce to a $50 fine or ninety days. Our case ended at
that point. Because the deadline for the fine was set
for October 31, 1973, it is assumed that Joyce paid it.

Case Analysis of a Drug Addict 2

Joyce, in contrast to Frank (in the preceding
case history), had been a heroin addict who supported
her habit through crime. Joyce had tried the therapeutic community approach to treating her problem; however, she was not emotionally strong enough to with-
stand the pressures put upon her by the program.

It was not until her third year of probation
supervision that Joyce demonstrated a relapse to drug
use. When an addict is under probation supervision and
not in an accompanying drug program, the chances of our
detecting resumed drug use are slight. If the addict
is in a drug program, urine analysis will usually dis-
close "secret" drug use (e.g., drug use going on not
perceived by others). Another way in which resumed
drug use would come to our attention is through a re-
arrest. There also exists the possibility that a member of the family might report drug use to us. This
was the case for Joyce, as her mother was our inform-
ant. Were it not for Mrs. F., we probably would not
have seen any signs of drug use during our brief contacts with Joyce. It has been stated earlier that
"secret deviants" exist where society fails to perceive
the rule-breaking behavior. Joyce's case shows us how
easy it would be to allow probation supervision to terminate without our knowing that the undesirable behavior persisted. Joyce's case also demonstrates how a
relapse to drug use can take its time to recur. For
all we know, if Frank (in the preceding case history)
were under our jurisdiction for his full length of probation, he could have shown the relapse too.

When it was discovered that Joyce was apparently
re-involved with drugs, the probation officer's response was to confront Joyce with the information and
to direct her to resume drug treatment. However, Joyce

sought to test our authority by refusing to keep appointments and by denying drug involvement. It is possible that in her third year of probation supervision, Joyce found the P-S process to be losing the initial threat that it once maintained for her. She probably also saw some refuge in the fact that the case was due for termination in a few months. The P-S process, however, invokes sanctions regardless of how much time remains until scheduled termination of probation. The practice of the court to pronounce a "declaration of delinquency" allows the probation period to stand still until the violation of probation is ruled upon. Joyce may not have realized these factors, as they were never explicitly made known to her. She, therefore, tested the P-S process and received a negative reinforcer, a violation of probation.

The outcome of Joyce's violation of probation was affected by an organizational factor of the court system--the delay in serving warrants. Had Joyce appeared in court immediately, she might have faced an alternative between re-entering a drug program or entering prison. As it turned out, by the time Joyce appeared in court and was referred to the probation officer for a progress report, there were no indications of drug use. We, therefore, operated along a particularistic consideration and recommended termination of probation. The court did not contradict us very much by its decision, as the fine imposed was slight. If the P-S process had not allowed for particularistic treatment, the court would have resentenced Joyce to incarceration. The slight punishment that Joyce received (the fine) is not sufficient to deter her from continuing the undesirable behavior of drug use. In a sense, when Joyce tested the P-S process she found that it does exercise its power; however, such power is belittled when the P-S process does not use the ultimate sanction of incarceration.

Case History of a Nonviolent Sex Offender

In October of 1973, Peter M. (age thirty-one) was placed on a three-year period of probation supervision for the charges endangering the welfare of a child and public lewdness. Specifically, the arrest was brought about by the complaint of a female who charged that while she was babysitting for two small children at a public swimming pool, Peter had exposed his private parts and manipulated his penis in front of the woman and children. Peter denied the allegations, claiming

126

that it was a case of mistaken identity. Peter claimed
that he had seen a "suspicious" gentleman at the scene
just as Peter had arrived. Peter advised the probation
officer that he had gone to the swimming pool to give
his stepdaughter spending money. He brought his thirteen-year old stepdaughter with him to the office to
attest to the fact that moments before Peter had been
arrested, he had given his stepdaughter's friend a mes-
sage for his stepdaughter to come out of the pool to
come over to him. Peter advised the probation officer
that his legal aid attorney would appeal the conviction.

During the probation presentence investigation,
the probation officer ascertained the following personal history for Peter: Peter was the product of a
broken home wherein his parents separated in 1957. His
mother died six months before the probation officer's
first contact with Peter. His father was living with a
common-law wife. His stepfather remained on good terms
with Peter. There were seven stepbrothers in the
family, but only the youngest one had actually grown up
in the same home with Peter. Peter's ex-wife was twen-
ty-eight years old. She was reportedly promiscuous;
however, Peter stated that the reason for the divorce
was because his wife had wanted to work and not rear a
family. They had three children: a boy (age six), a
girl (age eight), and another boy (age ten). Peter now
had the ten-year old boy with him. He suspected that
the two other children were actually not his. After
his ex-wife left him, she became pregnant by her boyfriend and gave birth to another boy. She was being
supported by public assistance. Peter's present common-law wife was six years older than he. He had known
her for several years and succeeded in winning her from
her former common-law husband. She had formerly been
legally married in Puerto Rico after an elopement.
This resulted in a divorce. Her seventeen-year old son
of that union was being reared by her mother in Puerto
Rico. Peter advised the probation officer that he regularly sent money there for support on behalf of her.
Peter used to support his own ex-wife, but stopped after two years. He had been together with his present
common-law wife for three years and was thinking about
a legal marriage. Those children who were in the
household were the thirteen-year old stepdaughter and
Peter's ten-year old son from his first marriage.
Peter advised the probation officer that his common-law
wife had a hysterectomy eight years before, but was in
good health except for an expected eye operation. The

family had been living in a low-income housing project for the past two years. Peter was employed as a machine operator in a knitting factory. The job was new; however, he had been in this line of work for several years.

There was an arrest history (which referred to, among other charges, a rape and an indecent exposure). When questioned about the circumstances of each of his prior arrests, Peter gave the following version. On February 13, 1959, he was charged with rape. According to Peter, a girlfriend claimed that she was pregnant by Peter. She was a minor. Her mother tried to get Peter to marry the girl. She was later found not to be pregnant. The charge was dismissed. On July 21, 1963, Peter was arrested for felonious assault. According to Peter, he was at a bar when a woman was annoying him. She put her hand in his pocket; and he broke a bottle over her head. He was acquitted of the charge. On September 21, 1966, Peter was arrested for indecent exposure. According to Peter, he was on a subway train and was somewhat intoxicated when he decided to urinate in between subway cars. A woman thought he was exposing himself to her and she yelled for police. He received a jail sentence of ten days.

With the above information known, we requested an examination by the court psychiatrist. We submitted a copy of our investigation to the court clinic along with the following reason for requesting the examination:

> In def't's. family history there are indications of events which could lead to confused sexual response, i.e., his former wife's promiscuity during marriage, his parents' separation, his common-law wife's inability to have any more children, etc. Def't. may be in need of therapy. We are interested in ascertaining whether the def't. can function in the community on probation with therapy and whether he is amenable to therapy.

We received a psychiatric report indicating a recommendation for probation supervision. According to the psychiatrist, therapy was not needed, although Peter had indicated that he would cooperate if required to undergo therapy. We recommended to the court that Peter be placed on probation supervision with the condition that he cooperate with a referral for therapy, if indicated. (This left the referral at the discretion of the supervising probation officer.) The court ordered the same.

The case was assigned to another probation officer for the entire supervision period. (This probation officer's supervisor would not allow a female to supervise male sex offenders.) This probation officer had an occasion to consult the case record approximately one year later and speak with the supervising probation officer. In that way, this probation officer was able to learn of the outcome of the case. It should be noted that it was for purely coincidental reasons that the probation officer looked at the case a year later. Peter had been living next door to a Child Neglect case of this probation officer's, as was discovered when he was encountered while the probation officer was knocking on the neighbor's door. At that time, the probation officer had a brief but informative conversation with Peter about his next door neighbors. Afterwards, the probation officer looked up Peter's case to see how much time he had remaining on probation, as it was thought that the probation officer might have Peter's supervising probation officer subtly find out some more information about the next-door neighbors. In formulating this plan, it was learned from the supervising probation officer that there had been no recurring incidents in Peter's case. There had been no need for a referral to therapy. Peter had been "laid off" from work; but there were no reported social problems in his living arrangements. He was due to be discharged from probation (early) after his next upcoming appointment with his probation officer. Although this probation officer cannot report first-hand on Peter's adjustment while on probation, his case record shows his supervision period as virtually uneventful.

Case Analysis of a Nonviolent Sex Offender

The analysis of Peter's response to the P-S process is brief, as this probation officer's contacts with him were during the presentencing phase, not the supervision phase of his case. Peter represents an individual with an emotional disturbance which manifests itself through his exposing his private parts in public (to females). This type of individual is probably best served through the mental hygiene system. However, in the interest of the victims who can become, themselves, emotionally upset by his actions, the "flasher" needs the authority of the courts to curb his actions.

Victims of this crime are not inclined to report it due to its embarrassing nature. Therefore, the male-to-female "flasher" can be reinforced to continue his actions knowing that the victim is not likely to report him. The challenge of eluding apprehension might, in itself, be as much of a pleasure to the "flasher" as is the sight of the helpless victim. Rather than speculate about what motivates the indecent exposure, one can speculate about how this type of offender's actions can be minimally controlled by the P-S process.

The court's first recourse is to view this individual as one in need of psychiatric therapy. It follows then that a sentence of probation coupled with psychiatric therapy is appropriate. Our examining psychiatrist decided to make therapy optional in this case, although he did not support his recommendation with any reasons. If the individual is convicted of another case of indecent exposure while under probation supervision, the court can justify its decision to then incarcerate. The individual suffers no harm in admitting himself to therapy, since he can superficially cooperate with the therapist. The individual can continue to commit the offense, with his chances of apprehension being in his favor.

In Peter's case, more than a year and a half had gone by with no known recurrence. However, there is no way of knowing whether Peter continued the behavior and escaped a complaint.

Case History of a Statutory Rapist

In July of 1974, George R. (age twenty-two) was placed on probation supervision for a period of one year for the charge attempted endangering the welfare of a child. Specifically, the complainant was the mother of a fifteen-year old girl with whom George had admittedly had intercourse in his apartment. According to George, the girl had informed him that she was seventeen years old. George also explained that he had known the girl for one month and they were in love. George believed that the mother overheard the girl discussing the incident over the phone with a friend; and the mother, being "strict," took the action against the girl's wishes. George advised the probation officer that he would make no attempts to contact the girl. However, because he remained interested in her, he felt that he would resume his relationship with her when she was of age. The probation officer wrote to the deponent (the mother), asking her whether there had been any further contact between George and the daughter (and whether any future problems between the two were anticipated). The mother phoned to reply that, although George had not resumed contact with the girl, there was some concern that he might do so. The mother was advised that there would be a special condition of probation ordering George not to contact the girl. The mother was apprised of how she could report any future incidents to the probation officer. The special condition of probation ordered George not to contact the deponent or her daughter.

The probation officer ascertained the following personal history during the probation presentence investigation: George was residing with his twenty-five year old brother in an apartment in the same neighborhood that their parents lived in. George's father was a bus driver; and the mother worked in a bank. George's brother (with whom George was living) was a college graduate, employed as a computer programmer. George also had two younger brothers, one younger sister, and two older, married sisters. George had attended Metropolitan Area Community College where he had studied commercial art; and he had attended Metropolitan Area Senior College where he had studied music. He planned to return to Metropolitan Area Senior College to study photography and developing. George had begun a recent dispatcher's job for a photo lab. Previously he had held a number of part-time jobs. He continued to work as a cab driver.

George had two prior court involvements. When he was seventeen years old, George had been given a "desk appearance ticket" for criminal mischief, which reportedly had involved breaking windows. We received a report from the County B Criminal Court Youth Counsel Bureau indicating that after their contacts with George, from April of 1969 to July of 1969, they had recommended dismissal of the case, which the court so ordered. The next court involvement occurred on May 18, 1973 when George had been arrested for giving an undercover police officer two marihuana cigarettes during a rock concert at the suburban Coliseum. That case had been "Adjourned in Contemplation of Dismissal" for one year on July 27, 1973 and also on August 3,

1973. The probation officer called the clerk at the Suburban County court and was told that the court had planned to calendar the case in August of 1974 to have George appear to inform them of any convictions within the year. The probation officer informed them of our case and wrote them an official letter containing the same information.

With the above information known, we recommended probation supervision to insure against further contact between George and the deponent's daughter. The plan for supervision was simply to monitor George's behavior by asking him about it. It was felt that the deponent would contact the probation officer if there were any further problems with George.

While George was under our supervision, he was cooperative and reported for appointments regularly. George changed jobs and eventually was employed full-time as a cab driver. He took civil service exams for the Post Office and for the city (bus driver); and he was on waiting lists for these jobs. George did not return to college during this time period, but he remained hopeful of doing so in the future. George moved into his own apartment for more privacy. He showed the probation officer pay stubs and receipts for bills that he regularly paid, although his ability to support himself was not questioned. Regarding the pending case in Suburban County, George reportedly had received phone messages from a detective to return calls. However, George lost the detective's name and phone number, which George's brother had given him. George waited for another contact from the detective, but did not hear from him again. George was worried about that case re-opening, but claimed that he never heard from the court again.

The probation officer's main concern was George's relationship with the fifteen-year old girl. Oddly enough, it appeared that there were no further contacts between George and the girl. The probation officer heard from the mother once concerning the fact that the girl had absconded from home and, in general, had been presenting behavior problems. The probation officer checked with George, who had no contact with the girl; and this was reported back to the mother. The mother was also advised to file a Person In Need of Supervision petition in Family Court to obtain a warrant and further assistance.

Within several months after he was placed on probation supervision, George had begun a relationship with a new girlfriend who was eighteen years old. George advised the probation officer that it was a "serious" relationship. The girlfriend accompanied George to our waiting room continuously, including at his last appointment.

After one year concluded, George's probation supervision case terminated administratively in July of 1975. This probation officer had no further contact with George.

Case Analysis of a Statutory Rapist

George represents a stable young man who is not likely to come in contact again with the courts for any serious misconduct. George would not ordinarily have received a period of probation supervision for his offense. The purpose of George's supervision was to service the deponent in controlling the relationship between her fifteen-year old daughter and George. Probation supervision served to deter George from continuing further contact with the girl. In actuality the girl was apparently quite willing to continue to see George. Therefore, George had to feel threatened by the court to the extent that it would not be worth his while to succumb to the girl's wishes, which he apparently had shared.

The case could have resulted differently had George felt more strongly about continuing his relationship with the girl. Perhaps under other conditions, the benefits of continuing to see a fifteen-year old girl (with whom a defendant was in love) could outweigh the consequences.

It is probable that the court and the probation officer viewed George in a particularistic sense and felt that he was hurt by the arrest, while he, himself, did not plan to hurt anyone. It is, therefore, very difficult to conjecture as to what extent the P-S process would have implemented its reinforcement plan had George disobeyed the probation officer's directions. Fortunately, George chose not to challenge the court's right to forbid him from continuing his contacts with the girlfriend.

Case History of an Intoxicated Driver (Repeater)

In June of 1974, Jack M.'s probation supervision case was transferred to our office from South Carolina under the Inter-State Compact Agreement. Jack had been granted permission by South Carolina to move to our jurisdiction. Jack (age forty-two) was married, with three children ranging in age from seven to sixteen.

In South Carolina Jack had been convicted of "driving while under the influence of alcohol, third offense." He was given a three-year period of probation and a $500 fine to be paid within one year.

At the first interview with Jack this probation officer learned that there was a fourth arrest for driving under the influence, occurring in our Suburban County on June 1, 1974 (before Jack returned to court for sentencing in South Carolina). The arrest occurred as the result of a minor auto accident during the time period in which the South Carolina court had allowed Jack to come to our state to look for relocation arrangements and a job. Jack pled guilty to the charge, driving while impaired. When Jack was arrested in Suburban County, there was no F.B.I. check made to determine out-of-state arrests. Therefore, the matter was discussed in the judge's chambers where a $50 fine was imposed. Because Jack was not directly asked any questions on this topic, he did not volunteer the information to the South Carolina court when he returned there for sentencing. This probation officer related the information to South Carolina; however, the latest arrest did not constitute a violation of probation, because it occurred before Jack had been placed on probation. The actual resolution of the case, after several adjournments, occurred on November 1, 1974 after Jack had been placed under our supervision.

Through this probation officer's initial interview with Jack and through a home visit with his wife, it was learned that the family was barely supported by Jack's sporadic income. Jack had been a truck driver, but was only able to get "shape-up" work. He was working for a moving company, but was not needed every day. The family's furniture was in storage in South Carolina, as they could not afford to pay for moving expenses. While Jack's relatives were in South Carolina, his wife's relatives were in Metropolitan Area. Mrs. M.'s relatives had already lent Jack any money that they were able to afford. The family never had any savings. Jack had spent most of his married life in the service. After the service, he had held sporadic truck driving jobs. Jack admittedly had an alcoholic problem for several years and was subject to periods of regression. Mrs. M. advised the probation officer that Jack was aware that Mrs. M. would end their marriage of eighteen years if Jack began drinking again. Although there was no specific condition on Jack's orders of probation requiring alcoholic treatment, the probation officer ordered Jack to admit himself into such treatment. The plan for probation supervision, therefore, included frequent contact, verification of alcoholic treatment, verification of earnings, and frequent collateral visits with Mrs. M. who was viewed as cooperative enough to report any misbehavior on the part of her husband. Jack was also viewed as very cooperative.

Jack reported regularly for appointments, was overly polite, and prepared to show all required verification. Jack was earning enough money to pay bills and rent, etc. He switched employment several times due to "lay offs." Jack immediately enrolled in the City Hospital's antabuse program. Mrs. M. dispensed an antabuse pill to Jack each morning.

On December 4, 1974, Jack was given a traffic citation in Suburban County. Jack had been charged with driving without a license (not driving while under the influence). It seems that Jack had a slip of paper notifying him that his application for a Metropolitan State driver's license renewal was acceptable and that his temporary driver's license was being returned to him (having been held by the court during the previous arrest). Jack claimed to have misunderstood the meaning of the notice. He thought that he was allowed to drive while possessing the notice. When Jack reported to court to answer the traffic offense, the court reportedly could not locate any papers for the reported case. This probation officer had no way of pursuing the matter, because our office had no official report of it; and it had happened outside the city's jurisdiction limits.

For the next few months, the alcoholic problem seemed to be cared for. However, the family's finances were minimal. Jack was out of work and ineligible for Unemployment Insurance Benefits. Jack was too proud to apply for public assistance, but the probation officer finally convinced him to do so. The probation officer assisted Jack with his application for emergency public assistance and had to give him a few dollars from our own office welfare fund. At this time, payment of the $500 fine in South Carolina was due. The probation officer wrote to the authorities in South Carolina explaining the above circumstances and was able to get a six-month extension of time.

Eventually, Jack began a cab driving job. On his third night out with the cab, he reportedly got in the way of an auto chase and was hurt seriously when a car collided with his cab. No charges were pressed against Jack. The other car left the scene. Jack suffered a neck and back injury causing him to wear a neck brace. He also suffered a chest injury where the steering wheel had bruised him. The cab company's attorney was in charge of determining hospital and disability insurance benefits. Jack filed a claim for workman's compensation; however, he was told that it would take an indefinite period of at least six weeks to assess his claim. Jack applied for public assistance, but was ineligible in view of his workman's compensation claim.

The next regression to occur was a bar fight. Mrs. M. had no control over Jack, as he was in a bad mood because of finances. He was not taking his antabuse regularly. In July of 1975, Jack went to a neighborhood bar (reportedly for the first time) and became intoxicated. He got into a physical altercation with the bar's owner. Jack was arrested for assault. This was his first criminal offense in Metropolitan Area's jurisdiction. The case was adjourned with hopes of the complaint being dropped. At this point Mrs. M. wanted a marital separation, if for no other reason she could receive support from the Department of Social Services if Jack was put out of the home by her. Jack stayed with Mrs. M.'s brother in County A, but was only welcomed there for a couple of days until he could make other arrangements. The probation officer suggested that Jack seek an emergency admission to the Veteran's Administration Hospital for alcoholic inpatient care. He was agreeable, as was Mrs. M. who accepted him back in the home temporarily. The probation officer supplied Jack with a letter of referral to the V.A. Hospital. Mrs. M. was given a letter of referral for emergency Aid to Dependent Children welfare assistance. On the day that Jack was supposed to report for an admission interview to the V.A. Hospital, he somehow was able to get enough money to become intoxicated and ride the subway all day. He finally found his way home; and Mrs. M. took him on the next day to the V.A. Hospital.

He was admitted on July 31, 1975 for an indefinite period. Mrs. M. later reported that Jack was also receiving good medical attention for his injuries that had been sustained in the previously mentioned car accident.

The probation officer wrote to South Carolina explaining the above incidents and again reporting to them that Jack would not be able to pay the fine on the upcoming due date. We were awaiting an answer from South Carolina when Jack was released from the V.A. Hospital on September 25, 1975. He was to report to the V.A. Hospital for a more elaborate plan of outpatient treatment than he had been receiving at the City Hospital. Jack was optimistic about his future abstinence from alcohol and about possibly rejoining his family. He was not accepted back into his wife's home. Jack appeared to be ready to seek employment. He would have been eligible for the Department of Social Service's Aid to the Disabled, in view of his recent hospital discharge to an alcoholic outpatient clinic; however, the workman's compensation case had not yet been resolved. Jack was due in court in November of 1975 for the assault case, which the complainant indicated that he wanted to drop.

At this time the case was transferred to another probation officer, because this probation officer was resigning from the agency. This probation officer had no further knowledge of Jack's progress after the last contact with him in October of 1975.

Case Analysis of an Intoxicated Driver (Repeater)

Jack represents an individual willing to undergo behavioral change when he is faced with the behavior modification contingencies. Jack recognizes and follows the law-abiding behavior in every respect but one --traffic offenses under the influence of alcohol. He has no criminal intent, but does have criminal negligence when he drives while under the influence of alcohol. The alleged fight in the bar appears to have been an isolated incident. Jack has an alcoholic condition, the source of which was not immediately known to the probation officer. The P-S process cannot actually produce obedience where a medical condition mitigates against obedience. The P-S process refers such matters to the appropriate agency; and, through the obedience relationship, insures the probationer's cooperation with the outside agency. In Jack's case, he willingly

137

accepted a referral to an alcoholic clinic (and later accepted a referral to inpatient care). The antabuse program is, in itself, a form of behavior modification, "aversion therapy." With an antabuse tablet in his system, if Jack were to ingest alcohol, he would experience a violent chemical reaction within his sytem. To avoid this unpleasant experience, Jack abstained from alcoholic intake. Lacking enough willpower to abstain from alcohol, Jack agreed to have his wife administer the antabuse regularly. Mrs. M. had a vested interest in doing so, as she was very concerned about her husband's alcoholic condition. Jack was also aware of his wife's threat to leave him if he did not stop drinking. Jack, therefore, had three different behavior modification contingencies to insure behavioral change. He faced a violation of probation for another conviction. He faced an unpleasant physiological experience while under antabuse treatment. And he faced the loss of his wife and children for continued drinking.

In a case such as Jack's, a behavioral change takes place as long as the contingencies remain in effect. The longer the behavioral change is sustained, the better are the chances for attitudinal change to occur. Under the doctrine of "soft determinism," it is possible for outside forces to block the individual's goal of behavioral change. Jack found himself experiencing a stream of bad luck surrounding his financial circumstances. His inability to support his family properly was disturbing to Jack. His auto accident and the resulting injury aggravated the situation that Jack found himself in. It was during his convalescence from the auto accident that Jack had stopped taking the antabuse. In the frame of mind that Jack was in while unemployed and ineligible for public assistance, he probably felt that he was worth little to his family. He did jeopardize his position with his family by resuming drinking. The re-arrest for assault in the bar occurred, in turn. He faced a violation of probation if the re-arrest would result in a conviction. Mrs. M. implemented her form of "omission" in the behavior modification scheme by the marital separation. The court consequences of the re-arrest were uncertain. With one of the three contingencies in effect, and a second one possibly due to come about, Jack was motivated to seek a more comprehensive form of help. It was then that he admitted himself for inpatient alcoholic care.

An alcoholic, like a drug addict, has a physical dependency on a substance. The physical dependency can be expected to compete with any promised reform, and can even be expected to succeed in causing relapse. Reinforcement methods are very much a part of an alcoholic's private world. He/she experiences positive reinforcement from the "high" while intoxicated. He/she experiences punishment from the "morning after" effects of overindulgence that replace the "high." He/she experiences omission through the loss of friends and relatives. If the alcholic experiences punishment and omission to a greater extent than he/she experiences positive reinforcement, he/she may be more amenable to receiving help from an outside threat, such as the P-S process. For Jack, the P-S process was somewhat hampered by technicalities that did not allow us to help have Jack's driving privileges revoked. This factor may have reflected upon an area in which we lacked authority. However, our authority to file a violation of probation upon a conviction of an offense was never doubted by Jack. If the complainant in the assault case later decided to drop the charge (as was indicated), the threat of that violation of probation would be removed. One can conjecture that even if a violation of probation had been sustained, the probation officer would not have recommended incarceration for Jack. Operating within the context of particularism, we would have recognized Jack's situation as calling for an alternative form of treatment. We probably would have asked for a modification of probation conditions to include residential, alcoholic treatment for a specific length of time. We could have also included a special condition of probation to forbid Jack to operate a motor vehicle. The probation department in South Carolina had the ultimate say in a recommendation to the court. It is not clear that they would have operated in a particularistic sense, because it is the individual probation officer that makes these allowances; and it is the individual case supervisor who approves or disapproves of such recommendations.

As a concluding observation in Jack's case, it is felt that he could produce the desired behavioral change if given a long enough period of time (e.g., the full three years) interacting with the P-S process.

Notes

[1]Portions of the introductory remarks are contained in Joan Luxenburg, "Purposes and Limitations of Case Histories of Criminal Offenders," paper presented at the 29th meeting of the American Society of Criminology, Atlanta, Ga., 18 November 1977.

[2]Daniel Katkin, Drew Hyman, and John Kramer, Juvenile Delinquency and the Juvenile Justice System (North Scituate, MA.: Duxbury Press, 1976), p. 121.

[3]Erikson, p. 45.

[4]The diagram is replicated from Walter L. Wallace, ed., Sociological Theory (Chicago: Aldine Publishing Co., 1969), p. ix, labelled "The Components and Process of Scientific Sociology." The interdependence of theory and empirical generalizations upon one another is discussed by Wallace. Robert K. Merton had earlier discussed the support that theory provides to research and the support that research provides to theory. See Robert K. Merton, On Theoretical Sociology (New York: Free Press, 1967), pp. 139-71 wherein Merton presents two articles, "The Bearing of Sociological Theory on Empirical Research" and "The Bearing of Empirical Research on Sociological Theory."

[5]The term "professional criminal" has a special connotation to it given by Walter C. Reckless. Professionals are highly specialized, may have acquired their skills in conventional employment, and enjoy a comfortable lifestyle. Examples include art forgers, jewelry switchers, safecrackers, etc. See Reckless, pp. 53-77.

[6]See Haskell and Yablonsky, pp. 22-29. The fourth and fifth categories of laws were not used. These are laws enacted to deter social change and laws enacted to promote social change. These categories include support of dependents laws and the Pure Food and Drug Act, respectively. The writer had no opportunity to work with cases in these categories.

[7]"Victimless crimes" usually are defined as crimes wherein either the victim and perpetrator are one and the same person; or the victim willingly engages in a mutual exchange of prohibited goods or services with the perpetrator. Examples are drug addiction (as per

the first definition) and prostitution (as per the second definition).

[8]Two separate case histories of drug addicts are provided. The type of drug being used is one rationale for the distinction. Other reasons will be discussed later. The first drug addict is involved in methadone; the second, in heroin.

[9]Clinard and Quinney, pp. 14-21.

[10]Ibid., p. 16.

[11]Gibbons, pp. 98-125.

[12]Ibid., p. 98.

[13]Ibid., p. 112.

[14]Ibid., p. 104.

[15]Ibid., p. 116.

[16]Ibid., p. 117.

[17]Ibid.

[18]William McCord and Arline McCord, American Social Problems (St. Louis: C.V. Mosby Co., 1977), chap. 8. See also Haskell and Yablonsky, chap. 11.

[19]Gibbons, p. 111.

[20]Edwin H. Sutherland, White Collar Crime, rev. ed. New York: Holt, Rinehart & Winston, 1961), pp. 9-10.

[21]Gibbons, p. 119.

[22]Ibid., p. 122.

[23]Ibid., p. 124.

[24]Other useful typologies are presented by Julian Roebuck, Criminal Typology: The Legalistic, Physical-Constitutional-Hereditary, Psychological-Psychiatric, and Sociological Approaches (Springfield, Ill: Charles C. Thomas, 1967); Alfred R. Lindesmith and H. Warren Dunham, "Some Principles of Criminal Typology," Social Forces 19 (March, 1941): 307-14; Ruth Shonle Cavan, Criminology, 3rd ed. (New York: Thomas E. Crowell Co., 1962), chap. 3. For a synopsis-discussion of the ty-

pological approaches, see Edwin I. Megargee, "Crime and Delinquency," in Deviants: Voluntary Actors in a Hostile World, ed. Edward Sagarin and Fred Montanino (N.p.: General Learning Press, 1977), pp. 40-56.

Chapter V

CONCLUSION

In this remaining chapter the writer's efforts are summarized to determine the extent to which the purposes of the study have been accomplished. The work constitutes a case study of the probation-supervision process. Knowledge of the methods of probation case-work (investigation and supervision functions) is a product of the writer's first-hand observation and participation in a large urban area's department of probation, although that agency is unaware of its contribution to this study. Information regarding the socialization process was obtained through a selected review of the literature which deals with the major models that can explain the learning of societal-approved behavior.

The specific goals of the study were formalized in introductory statements. Essentially, these were the following:

1. To intellectualize the role of a probation officer;

2. To show the probation-supervision process as an educative or reformative one, e.g., a system that resocializes lawbreakers;

3. To identify the dominant method of socialization relied upon by the probation-supervision process;

4. To formulate the probation-supervision model, accounting for its priorities, as well as for its limitations in outcome;

5. To provide illustrations (through case histories) of the application of the probation-supervision model;

6. To perform the therapeutic contribution of "reflectation" upon the potential client, the Metropolitan Area Department of Probation.

Intellectualizing the Role of a Probation Officer

To inform the reader of the assignments of the probation officer, e.g., his/her daily routine, his/her job atmosphere, etc., would be purely descriptive. Such a description is preliminary to further discussion of the probation-supervision system. However, intellectualizing the probation officer's role is quite a different technique. It requires reasoning or the drawing of inferences from known facts. It has been established that the manifest role of the probation officer is to resocialize the lawbreaker. One must, consequently, draw inferences from the facts which are known to be true of the probation officer's role, rather than from the writer's construction of the role. The latent functions of the probation officer's role were not being analyzed here, as that type of analysis could constitute an entire study of its own. The function of a probation officer is indisputable in view of the accepted definition of the term probation supervision. Operationally, probation supervision has been defined as a process whereby an individual who has been convicted of a crime is sentenced to a period of community surveillance and guidance under the aegis of a court-appointed probation officer.

The writer has drawn conclusions about the manifest role of the probation officer, after defining his/her function as that of a resocializer. It is at this point that the task of intellectualizing the role commenced. There was no other parameter involved in this particular goal of the study. The remainder of the study played a part at all times in continuing to reason out the role of the probation officer as an agent of resocialization. The probation officer has been shown to be an educator who implements models of learning to correct deficits in the lawbreaker's prior knowledge, ability, and motivation surrounding the society's expected behavior and values. In doing so, the probation officer is forced to minimize the importance of values, and thereby must accept the consequential superficial learning that he/she fosters.

Viewing the Probation-Supervision Process as an Educative or Reformative One

The "reformative" function of corrections has been operationally defined as "modifying deviant behavior (and attitudes and values) toward acceptable societal standards." Through further discussion, it has been shown that the P-S process emphasizes efforts to change unacceptable behavior, practically to the exclusion of any effort toward changing values. Educating or socializing an individual can be accomplished through behavioral change only. This has been shown to be the case for operant conditioning. The question arises as to whether such change will endure, given the possibility that the underlying values and attitudes may be operating in contradiction to the newly learned behavior. Removing the resocialization agent (probation officer) from the scene so that he/she no longer applies reinforcers (after the period of probation supervision expires) may detract from continued performance of desirable behavior on the part of the former probationer. In some cases, it seems likely that the known threat of consequences remains with the probationer deterring him/her from repetition of lawbreaking behavior. It is problematic as to whether or not the influence of the probation officer continues to operate (after the period of P-S has expired). The influence addresses itself to the behavioral change only. It is uncertain that any attitude or value change takes place at all.

Given the earlier discussion of the relative importance of knowledge, ability, and motivation in the socialization process, one has to question not only the P-S process, but any correctional practice in its reforming of deviants. As was earlier indicated, if society erroneously blames the deviant individual for motivational deficiencies, this eases the conscience of society; but it also makes genuine resocialization difficult to accomplish. However, where motivation is correctly identified as the true source of deviant behavior, it would seem that the educative devices that the P-S process employs, in motivating probationers to obey society's behavioral expectations, are used appropriately.

Identifying the Dominant Method of Socialization Relied Upon by the P-S Process

After having reviewed the major perspectives which explain the dynamics of socialization, reinforcement theory has been identified as that source upon which the method of the P-S process rests. For those instances where motivation is the source of deviant behavior, a reinforcement process (such as behavior modification) can aptly provide incentives and rewards for increasing law-abiding behavior and can provide deterrence in order to prevent continued lawbreaking behavior. Reinforcement makes use of one of mankind's most

145

basic motivational patterns--that of seeking the avoidance of pain and the maximization of pleasure. The specific contingencies that are made use of by the P-S process have been enumerated in the formulation of the P-S process model.

Formulating the Probation-Supervision Process Model

Table 9 specifies the priority, method, and outcome of the P-S process. The P-S process may be said to hold a priority of reforming the lawbreaker. However, the change brought about in the subject is somewhat superficial. The subject is said to have been reformed when he/she demonstrates that he/she knows the expected behavior. His/her motivation to carry out the expected behavior is the product of external mechanisms of control which have not necessarily led to a concomitant internalization of expected values. The P-S process model cannot work within the realm of nonobservable nonbehaviors (values), which are beyond its scope. The external forces which bring about the behavioral change are a composite of authority-based threats, incentives, and rewards. The authority is derived through an agreement between the probationer and the court. The power to enforce both negative and positive sanctions rests with the probation officer and the court. There is some room for mitigating circumstances to allow a reprieve to those who do not adhere to the commands of the P-S process. Other than these occasional allowances for particularistic treatment, the system impersonally applies its negative sanctions. The P-S process follows through on its promises of rewards and on its threats of punishments. But this practice constitutes the only form of validating societal norms that the P-S process has some reasonable assurance of accomplishing. As a consequence, if any learning is to take place, it is an opportunistic learning, rather than an internalization of the norms.

The Use of Case Histories to Illustrate the Application of the P-S Process Model

The writer has qualified, for the reader, the use of case-history presentation in participant-observation research. For the writer's purposes, the case histories are meant to be anecdotal. Using an array of types of adult offenders, the writer was able to furnish examples of the P-S process implementing its priority and method. Simultaneously, the case histories were able to illustrate the offenders' responses to the

146

P-S process--the equivalent concept of the "outcome" of the P-S process. Each case-history analysis focused upon some interactions that would support the formulated P-S process model. Undoubtedly, the reader was not able to find all of the elements of the model operating in any one case; however, after combining the transactions that had taken place in all ten cases, the reader is given an opportunity to recognize all of those elements contained in the model--its priority, method, and outcome.

Reflectation

The writer had promised at the outset to perform the therapeutic service of "reflectation" upon the client, the probation-supervision process. More precisely, the potential client is the Metropolitan Area Department of Probation; but the writer's intent was not to spotlight one department of probation. The Metropolitan Area Department of Probation was used because it is the setting in which the writer was able to gather knowledge of the P-S process.

To remind the reader of the analogous use of the term "reflectation," it would be best to explain the common use of reflection by psychotherapists and counselors. The following dialogue could take place between a client and therapist:

Client: "My wife and I have been arguing constantly every day during this past week."

Therapist: "I take it that you and your wife are having your differences."

What the therapist has done here is to repeat the client's expressed thoughts, without imparting meaning to them, but by merely paraphrasing them. This process is "reflecting." It allows the client to know that the therapist has understood what the client is trying to express. Reflecting also is a response that facilitates a continuation of the client's information-giving. As the dialogue continues, the therapist's responses may then begin to impart meaning to the client's thoughts and behavior. If so, then interpretation has begun:

Client: "My wife is leaving me."

Therapist: "How do you feel about that?"

Client: (Angrily) "I don't care. If she wants to go, let her go. She will suffer; not me."

Therapist: "You seem upset."

Client: "Well, of course, I'm upset. How would you feel in my position?"

Therapist: "I would be upset . . . if I did not want the marriage to end."

(Pause)

Therapist: "You say that she can go if she wants to go. But you are upset. So, you don't really mean that you don't care about her leaving--do you?"

At the pause, the interpretation has taken place. The therapist hypothesizes a set of relationships between the client's signs of anger, nervousness, despair, etc., to indicate that the thought of the wife's leaving was upsetting to the client and was, therefore, against the client's wishes. But the client had begun by stating that his wife's plans did not bother him. The client's behavior in the therapist's office contradicted his previous statements. In the last statement, the therapist blends the reflection and the interpretation. He/she then confronts the client with the obvious discrepancy and subjects the contradiction to the client for his own review. If the dialogue were to proceed further, perhaps the next step that the client would be forced to take (for cognitive consonance) is to change either his early statement or his behavior. He is going to do something to reconcile his own contradiction that the therapist has pointed out to him. If the client relieves the inconsistency, his doing so will pave the way for him to see reality less confusingly, and to learn to cope with his presenting problem.

In the analogy, this writer is taking the role of the therapist. The probation-supervision process is the potential client. The study first "reflected" or repeated the client's thoughts, e.g., how socialization takes place. The selected socialization literature presented in Chapter II is agreed upon by the P-S process. The use of external mechanisms of control is heavily relied upon by the P-S process to reform lawbreakers. The correctional system (which includes probation supervision) feels that the reformative function accomplishes a change in behavior, attitudes, and values. Thus, the P-S process is professing to be able to change the behavior, attitudes, and values of those offenders that it successfully works with.

In Chapter III the writer has "interpreted" the priority, method, and outcome of the P-S process by formulating the model. The validity of the exposition set forth in the model is, of course, subject to disagreement by others. It is the writer's construct, representing the writer's own inferences drawn from six years of participant observation. If the interpretation is correct, the case histories presented in Chapter IV should illustrate and sustain the model rather than contradict it. In Chapter IV, the writer has covered any questionable aspects of personal influence upon the case histories, as well as any questions concerning the selection of case histories. The degree of behavioral interactions within the case histories is unavoidably weak, due to what has been referred to as "organizational constraints."

The blending of "reflection" and "interpretation" concludes this study. Comments will be directed first to the element of the model referred to as priority; then method; and, lastly, outcome.

In a sense, the client believes that, of those cases that it can successfully work with, the P-S process reforms lawbreakers. The P-S process, therefore, professes to change the behavior, attitudes, and values of its successful cases. One has as a measure of case success its termination under favorable conditions (either at its scheduled expiration date; or through requested early, "improved" termination). Alternatively, an unsuccessful case is one that results in a sustained violation of probation (whether due to a conviction for a re-arrest or due to an infraction of the orders of probation). Firstly, one can challenge whether any true knowledge of a probationer's changed attitudes and values can be established. The concept of behavioral change can be demonstrated. However, there is some question about the durability of the demonstrated behavioral change. If desired behavioral change is demonstrated during the period of probation supervision, there is no assurance that the new behavior will endure after the termination of probation supervision. Chapter IV contained a case history of each of two drug addicts. One case terminated early (after one year of the three-year sentence had been served). It was considered a "successful" termination. Had the probation officer decided to terminate the other drug addict's case early (after a period of one year), her case would have been termed a "success." However, this second case resulted in "failure" during the end of the third year of probation supervision. Similarly, when other cases were terminated earlier than scheduled (for budgetary reasons), these cases were being labelled "successes." In actuality these cases may not have been successes in terms of the working definition of the reformative function of probation supervision.

The above reflectation directed itself to the element of priority entailed in the P-S process. The next exercise in reflectation addresses itself to the method employed by the P-S process. It has already been determined that an authority-based relationship exists in probation supervision. It results from a signed agreement between the probationer and the court. Whether or not the probation officer reiterates the threat behind the authority, the probationer may be resentful of the element of authority. When the probation officer uses authority, the obedience that results may be more a consequence of feelings of conflict than of feelings of conformity. The feelings held by the probationer toward the probation officer (and toward the court) may result in embitterment toward society's expected behavior and values. Thus, the method that works best for immediate, overt behavioral change may be the very same method that counteracts feelings of "identification" conducive to the internalization of these standards. Another point to be made with regard to the method of probation supervision encompasses particularistic treatment. If the parameters for "special" treatment are properly controlled, there would not be an excessive use of "favored" treatment of cases. Too much use of particularism would undermine the system. Some would criticize the case history of an intoxicated driver as having been treated too lax. Certainly, if the intoxicated driver perceived the P-S process as being weak in invoking authority, he would not be deterred. He would be a likely candidate to physically hurt himself or others in a criminally negligent auto accident.

The use of laxity may not necessarily stem from a weak probation officer, but may instead be the result of an organizational constraint. Unfortunately, in this case study, the city suffered a budget crisis that created a new criterion for early termination of a case. This practice was used temporarily, and was thereafter discontinued. This "emergency" termination has been referred to in several of the case histories, wherein eligibility was determined if a new court conviction had not taken place during a specified portion of the probation sentence. An example of another organizational constraint--excessive caseloads--was referred to in Chapter III. It is possible for individual probation officers to submit cases to court for early termination, simply to relieve their own volume of cases. Under these circumstances cases that do not warrant early termination could be convincingly presented to the court in such a manner whereby the court grants the early termination.

Thus, two contradictions in the method of probation supervision are most evident. The first is the possibility that the use of authority evokes feelings of resentment toward societal expectations. The second is the alternative--showing the probationer the laxity of the system, thus undermining its authority.

The final reflectation presented here deals with the outcome of probation supervision--the form of learning that takes place, if learning takes place at all. In the model, opportunistic learning was specified as the outcome of probation supervision. There is no contradiction in the model among the elements of priority (overt behavioral change), the method (reinforcement), and the outcome (opportunistic learning). The inconsistency lies in the idealistic view that the P-S process presents to society. Society is informed that probation supervision resocializes lawbreakers. Society views probation supervision as a method of correcting previously learned patterns of offender behavior in favor of newly learned patterns of law-abiding behavior. Society desires that the new pattern of behavior will permanently replace the old pattern. If "propriate" learning were the outcome of the P-S process, internalization of standards would give more assurance of the permanence of the resocialization. Opportunistic learning will have to suffice, and probably can produce lasting results in an undetermined proportion of cases. The offender in the case history of white-collar employee theft probably learned not to repeat the offense; but she probably did not learn that the offense was inherently wrong. One is reminded of Kohlberg's belief that most of us respond morally "by convention," not "on principle." As long as society is aware of the possibility that the learning outcome of the P-S process, for the most part, is not necessarily internalized, the P-S system can serve as our host, providing us with protection.

Those who represent the P-S process, e.g., administrators and practitioners, are the medium through which the public receives its information about the purposes and accomplishments of probation supervision. The first step in information-processing about the P-S process begins with the administrators and practitioners admitting the system's limitations. With this accomplished, those in the field can cope with the system and perhaps strive for its improvement. (This is analogous to the hypothetical client who saw reality through the help of the therapist.)

While the study was confined to the importance of the probation officer's knowledge of socialization, it is recognized that there are other areas of equal importance in which probation officers ought to be knowledgeable. The content of discussions between the probation officer and his/her clients will differ among probation officers. However, the process which guides these contacts remains uniform. The P-S process, in a sense, is the actual subject matter discussed between the probation officer and his/her client. Undoubtedly, a probation officer with a strong academic training in psychology will be approaching topics with his/her client somewhat differently than would a probation officer with a strong background in the study of criminal justice. Each probation officer brings into his/her casework interactions an area of expertise based primarily upon prior academic training and orientation. However, the system in which each probation officer operates is shared by all probation officers regardless of their preference of one academic discipline over another. One might assume that the best prepared probation officer is the one who brings with him/her a composite of skills from the disciplines of the behavioral sciences, criminal justice, and social work. This may be the optimal combination of skills; and yet the diversity may or may not succeed as well as a particular specialization of academic knowledge. The writer dares not specify here which academic discipline is more successful than others as a preparation for probation casework. The concern is not with the specific "world view" that each probation officer holds. The concern is that probation officers know how the process of resocialization takes place, and continue to improve upon their use of the process.

BIBLIOGRAPHY

Allport, Gordon. _Becoming_. New Haven: Yale University Press, 1955.

Allport, Gordon and Postman, Leo. _The Psychology of Rumor_. New York: Holt, Rinehart & Winston, 1947.

Asch, Solomon. "Studies of Independence and Conformity I. A Minority of One Against a Unanimous Majority." _Psychological Monographs_ 70 (1956): whole no.

Bandura, Albert. "Influence of models' reinforcement contingencies on the acquisition of imitative responses." _Journal of Personality and Social Psychology_ 1 (1965): 589-95.

_____. _Principles of Behavior Modification_. New York: Holt, Rinehart & Winston, 1969.

Bandura, Albert, and Walters, Richard. _Social Learning and Personality Development_. New York: Holt, Rinehart & Winston, 1963.

Baron, Robert A., and Byrne, Donn. _Exploring Social Psychology_. Boston: Allyn and Bacon, 1979.

_____. _Social Psychology: Understanding Human Interaction_. 3rd ed. Boston: Allyn and Bacon, 1981.

Becker, Howard S. _The Outsiders_. New York: Free Press, 1963.

Brammer, Lawrence M., and Shostrom, Everett L. _Therapeutic Psychology_. 3rd ed. Englewood Cliffs, N.J.: Prentice-Hall, 1977.

Brim, Orville G., Jr. "Socialization Through the Life Cycle." In _Socialization After Childhood_, pp. 3-49. Edited by Orville G. Brim, Jr., and Stanton Wheeler. New York: John Wiley & Sons, 1966.

California (State of) Adult Authority, Division of Adult Paroles. _Special Intensive Parole Unit_. Sacramento: State of California, 1953.

Campbell, Ernest Q. *Socialization: Culture and Personality*. Dubuque: Wm. C. Brown Co., 1975.

"Caseload Has Little Impact on Recidivism." *Law Enforcement Assistance Administration Newsletter*, 6 September 1977, p. 11.

Cavan, Ruth Shonle. *Criminology*. 3rd ed. New York: Thomas E. Crowell Co., 1962.

Chamber of Commerce of the United States of America. *Marshaling Citizen Power to Modernize Corrections*. Reprinted by American Correctional Association. College Park: American Correctional Association, 1972.

Clinard, Marshall B., and Quinney, Richard. *Criminal Behavior Systems: A Typology*. 2nd ed. New York: Holt, Rinehart & Winston, 1973.

Cohen, Albert K. *Delinquent Boys*. Glencoe: Free Press, 1955.

Cooley, Charles Horton. *Human Nature and the Social Order*. New York: Scribner's, 1902.

Cullen, Francis T., and Gilbert, Karen E. *Reaffirming Rehabilitation*. Cincinnati: Anderson Publishing Co., 1982.

Dreeben, Robert. *On What Is Learned in School*. Reading, MA.: Addison-Wesley Publishing Co., 1968.

Erikson, Erik. *Childhood and Society*. 2nd ed. New York: W. W. Norton & Co., 1963.

Festinger, Leon. *A Theory of Cognitive Dissonance*. Evanston, Ill.: Row Peterson, 1957.

Festinger, Leon, and Carlsmith, J. M. "Cognitive Consequences of Forced Compliance." *Journal of Abnormal and Social Psychology* 58 (1959): 203-10.

Freud, Sigmund. *An Outline of Psychoanalysis*. Translated by J. Strachey. New York: Norton, 1949.

Gibbons, Don C. *Changing the Lawbreaker: The Treatment of Delinquents and Criminals*. Englewood Cliffs, N.J.: Prentice-Hall, 1965.

Haskell, Martin, and Yablonsky, Lewis. Criminology: Crime and Criminality. 2nd ed. Chicago: Rand McNally, 1978.

Inkeles, Alex. "Social Structure and the Socialization of Competence." Harvard Eduational Review 36 (1963): 265-83.

Katkin, Daniel, Hyman, Drew, and Kramer, John. Juvenile Delinquency and the Juvenile Justice System. North Scituate: Duxbury Press, 1976.

Kennedy, Daniel B., and Kerber, August. Resocialization: An American Experiment. New York: Behavioral Publications, 1973.

Kohlberg, Lawrence. "Moral Stages and Moralization." In Moral Development and Behavior: Theory, Research, and Social Issues, pp. 31-53. Edited by Thomas Lickona. New York: Holt, Rinehart & Winston, 1976.

Lazerson, Arlyne, ed. Psychology Today: An Introduction. New York: Random House, 1975.

Lerner, Mark J. "The Effectiveness of a Definite Sentence Parole Program." Criminology 15 (August, 1977): 211-24.

Lindesmith, Alfred R., and Dunham, H. Warren. "Some Principles of Criminal Typology." Social Forces 19 (March, 1941): 307-14.

Luxenburg, Joan. "Purposes and Limitations of Case Histories of Criminal Offenders." Paper presented at the 29th meeting of the American Society of Criminology, Atlanta, Ga., 18 November 1977.

_____. "Structural Provisions for Normative Learning: Traditional and Open Classrooms." Scholar and Educator (Fall, 1978): 22-30.

McCord, William, and McCord, Arline. American Social Problems. St. Louis: C. V. Mosby Co., 1977.

Matza, David. Delinquency and Drift. New York: John Wiley, 1966.

Mead, George Herbert. Mind, Self, and Society. Chicago: University of Chicago Press, 1934.

Megargee, Edwin I. "Crime and Delinquency." In <u>Deviants: Voluntary Actors in a Hostile World</u>, pp. 40-56. Edited by Edward Sagarin and Fred Montanino. N.p.: General Learning Press, 1977.

Merton, Robert K. <u>On Theoretical Sociology</u>. New York: Free Press, 1967.

Michigan Council on Crime and Delinquency. <u>The Saginaw Probation Demonstration Project</u>. Lansing: Michigan Council on Crime and Delinquency, 1963.

Muson, Howard. "Moral Thinking: Can It Be Taught." <u>Psychology Today</u> (February, 1979): 48-68, 92.

Pavlov, Ivan P. <u>Conditioned Reflexes</u>. New York: Macmillan, 1927.

Piaget, Jean. <u>The Moral Judgment of the Child</u>. Translated by M. Gabain. New York: Harcourt Brace Jovanovich, 1932.

_____. <u>The Origins of Intelligence in Children</u>. Translated by M. Cook. New York: International Universities Press, 1969.

Pincus, Allen, and Minahan, Anne. <u>Social Work Practice: Model and Method</u>. Itasca, Ill.: F. E. Peacock Publishing Co., 1973.

Reckless, Walter C. <u>The Crime Problem</u>. New York: Appleton-Century-Crofts, 1961.

Roebuck, Julian B. <u>Criminal Typology: The Legalistic, Physical-Constitutional-Hereditary, Psychological-Psychiatric and Sociological Approaches</u>. Springfield, Ill.: Charles C. Thomas Publishing Co., 1967.

Sandhu, Harjit S. <u>Modern Corrections</u>. Springfield, Ill.: Charles C. Thomas Publishing Co., 1974.

Sherif, Muzafer. "An Experimental Approach to the Study of Attitudes." <u>Sociometry</u> 1 (1937): 90-98.

Skinner, B. F. <u>Science and Human Behavior</u>. New York: Macmillan, 1953.

Skolnick, Jerome. <u>Justice Without Trial</u>. New York: John Wiley, 1966.

Smith, M. Brewster. "Competence and Socialization."
In Socialization and Society, pp. 272-320. Edit-
ed by John A. Clausen. Boston: Little, Brown &
Co., 1968.

Sorokin, Pitrim. Fads and Foibles in Modern Sociology.
Chicago: Henry Regnery Co., 1956.

Sutherland, Edwin H. White Collar Crime. Rev. ed. New
York: Holt, Rinehart & Winston, 1961.

Sutherland, Edwin H., and Cressey, Donald R. Criminology. 10th ed. Philadelphia: J. B. Lippincott
Co., 1978.

Sutton-Smith, Brian. Child Psychology. New York: Appleton-Century-Crofts, 1973.

Tharp, Roland G., and Wetzel, Ralph J. Behavior Modification in the Natural Environment. New York:
Academic Press, 1969.

University of California School of Criminology. The
San Francisco Project: A Study of Federal Proba-
tion and Parole. Research Report no. 14. Los
Angeles: University of California Press, 1969.

U. S. Department of Health, Education, and Welfare.
Children's Bureau. "Alternatives to Institutionalization," by Marguerite Q. Grant and Martin
Warren. In Children. Washington, D.C.: Government Printing Office, 1963.

Wallace, Walter L., ed. Sociological Theory. Chicago:
Aldine Publishing Co., 1969.

Wasserman, Harry. "The Professional Social Worker in a
Bureaucracy." Social Work 16 (January, 1971):
89-95.

ABOUT THE AUTHOR

Joan Luxenburg is an associate professor of sociology and criminal justice at Central State University in Edmond, Oklahoma. Previously, Dr. Luxenburg taught at Western Illinois University and in New York Institute of Technology's College Accelerated Program for Police. The author of articles on police higher education, police stress, and CB radio prostitution, Dr. Luxenburg holds an Ed.D. from Columbia University in sociology and education. Dr. Luxenburg is the author of two test manuals (to accompany introductory texts in sociology and American national government). Additionally, Dr. Luxenburg serves as a consulting editor to the journal FREE INQUIRY in Creative Sociology.